# PERFECT PASTA

*Triple-Pepper Fettuccini, page 41*

# PERFECT PASTA

RODALE

Printed in the United States of America
Rodale Inc. makes every effort to use acid-free ♾, recycled paper ♻.

*Cover photograph:* markthomasstudio.com
*Cover recipe:* Farfalle Primavera,
Courtesy of Colavita, page 45
*Food stylist:* Diane Vezza
*Illustrations:* Judy Newhouse

Produced by:
BETH ALLEN ASSOCIATES, INC.

*President/Owner:* Beth Allen
*Designer:* Monica Elias
*Art Production Director:* Laura Smyth (smythtype)
*Culinary Consultant/Food Editor:* Deborah Mintcheff
*Food Writer:* Jean Galton
*Copy Editor:* Brenda Goldberg
*Public Relations Consultants:* Stephanie Avidon, Melissa Moritz
*Nutritionist:* Michele C. Fisher, Ph.D., R.D.

**Library of Congress Cataloging-in-Publication Data**

Perfect pasta.
p. cm.
Includes index.
ISBN 1-57954-953-5 hardcover, tqc
ISBN 1-59486-063-7 hardcover, qtf
1. Cookery (Pasta) I. Rodale (Firm)
TX809.M17P47 2004
641.8'22—dc22 2003026226

2 4 6 8 10 9 7 5 3 1 hardcover, tqc
2 4 6 8 10 9 7 5 3 1 hardcover, qtf

RODALE
WE INSPIRE AND ENABLE PEOPLE TO IMPROVE THEIR LIVES AND THE WORLD AROUND THEM

# CONTENTS

# INTRODUCTION

## *Here's your fast answer to supper!*

Ever wish you would never have to wonder what's for supper again? That somehow, someone would invent the perfect, fast and easy solution to the daily dinner dilemma using what you already have on hand? That day has arrived! For right this very moment, you're holding 100 foolproof candidates for supper-in-a-flash. To get started, all you need is the quick-cooking recipes in *Perfect Pasta*—plus a box or bag of pasta, of course.

Quickly take a look at our collection of recipes. One of the first things you'll notice is that many are tagged *SuperQuick*. Choose these recipes, and you'll be in and out of the kitchen in thirty minutes or less—with dinner in hand. To guarantee you'll have the quickest pasta supper, reach for fresh pasta. There's a Shrimp Linguine Primavera (page 33) made faster with shrimp from your freezer and a speedy fresh Tortellini with Tomatoes & Zucchini (page 24), tossed quickly in a tomato sauce made from two cans from your pantry. Keep dried pastas on hand so you'll be able to try the fastest Chili Mac ever, made in one skillet (page 27) and a Italian Chicken Pasta (page 120).

We haven't forgotten the traditional dishes, too, such as that old friend Classic Mac & Cheese (page 56), Pasta with Homemade Meat Sauce (page 25), and an Easy Classic Lasagna (page 129). You'll discover we've also put that Italian favorite Hay & Straw (page 62), made from green and white linguine, on the fast track. Plus we've added some unusual pasta shapes, such as Michael's Pasta, which uses radiatore ("little radiators"), and even a Beef & Mozzarella Pie (page 132), just perfect for weekend entertaining.

Start off by reading the next chapter, "The Faster Pasta Pot." You'll find eight exciting new discoveries connected with buying, cooking, and saucing up pasta. Look on page 10 to find out how to cook pasta the no-fuss way—and how to make the best plate of pasta around, borrowed from our Italian friends.

But that's just the beginning. We've teamed up with test kitchens of famous food manufacturers and other cooking pros from coast to coast with one goal in mind: to bring you 100 fabulous, quick-cooking, flavor-packed pasta recipes. Many use fewer ingredients than your current recipes, without skimping on the flavor. All come kitchen-tested to ensure perfect results every time, even if you're not an accomplished cook. Some come with *On the Menu* ideas to help you plan dinner on a weekday or weekend, however little time you have.

Throughout this book, you'll find *Cooking Basics* sidebars filled with helpful information, such as how much pasta to put into the pot and the three quick steps to cooking perfect pasta. Have you ever made a perfect sauce, only to discover it slid right off of your pasta when you tried eating it? Take a peek at our feature box on page 11, and you'll find many different pastas—from the traditional fettuccine ribbons to little moustaches—and which types of sauces top them best. Plus we've created eleven different kinds of pronto-pasta suppers you can make from a jar of red sauce and a pound of pasta (page 12).

And that's not all. You'll find first-hand advice in our *Cook to Cook* boxes, which share quick-cooking tips from cooks just like you, such as how to tell when pasta is done. And in our *Microwaving in Minutes* boxes, you'll discover how pasta can be reheated to just-cooked freshness in the microwave. You'll also notice handy *Time Savers* sifted throughout the pages, with great tips, such as how to partially precook pasta for a crowd. And do you know how many gallons of water it takes to cook a billion pounds of pasta? Check out our *Food Facts* box on page 128.

*Perfect Pasta* has been created just for you to whip up 100 suppers in a flash, plus a wealth of high-speed kitchen hints. Enjoy reading and using them, while realizing you can look forward to even more great cooking ideas in the other books in our quick-cooking collection. Each book brings you exactly what you've told us you want in today's cookbooks—quick-cooking recipes, beautiful photographs, time-saving techniques that work, and handy tips. And just like the other books in the collection, we guarantee each one will soon become a "fast kitchen friend." We've created each book in our quick-cooking series to be not only enjoyable and fun to browse through but also so jam-packed with good food ideas that you'll find yourself referring to, and using, each one time and again. With so many great homemade (and better-tasting!) pasta recipes for everyday suppers, pasta tosses, garden fresh sauces, and weekend bakes, you'll soon find many delicious answers to "what's for supper tonight."

Here's to fabulous quick-cooking with pasta. Mangia!

*Michael's Pasta, page 67*

# The Faster Pasta Pot

Nothing could be faster, easier, or tastier than a plate of pasta. It's one of the easiest fast foods that goes from ordinary to extraordinary in a flash. Boil some fresh pasta, heat up a jar of sauce, choose one of our eight ways to make it special, then just enjoy. Dinner's ready in minutes! Here you'll also find seven no-fail secrets to making your next pasta pot—some from the Italians, others from cooks just like you. There's a no-fuss way to boil the pot, a no-stress way to throw a pasta party, and a no-cook way to stir up some fabulous sauces. Since pasta's so versatile, we even show which pasta to substitute for what. All the tips you need for making that perfect pot of pasta.

## THE FASTEST PASTA AROUND

With fresh pastas in your grocer's refrigerated section and handmade pastas available in specialty take-out boutiques, dinner from the pasta pot has never been so fast. Fresh pasta cooks more quickly than dried pasta, with ribbons and strands cooking in 1 to 2 minutes, stuffed pastas in 5 to 7 minutes. Watch them carefully (they can overcook in a flash!). There are fresh stuffed pastas, such as ravioli, manicotti, and tortellini, all either filled with wonderful stuffings or made from flavored doughs. And freshly cut long strands, such as fusilli, and ribbons, such as tagliatelle, fettuccine, or linguine.

## NO-FUSS PASTA COOKING

What's the best pot for cooking pasta in? A pasta cooker. It's a large stockpot-style pot with a colander insert that fits perfectly inside. Place the colander insert inside the pot. Add the water (about 4 quarts to a pound of pasta)and bring to a rolling boil. Drop the pasta into the colander, stir, and cook. When the pasta's ready, simply lift the insert holding the pasta and drain it over the pot. This eliminates carrying a heavy pot of boiling water to the sink.

## THE BEST DISH OF PASTA

Take a tip from the Italians—they love to finish cooking dried pastas the last few minutes in the sauce. First, cook the sauce in a pan large enough to hold the cooked pasta and sauce. Then, cook the pasta only three-quarters of the usual time. Drain it, saving 1 cup of the pasta cooking water. Put the pasta into the pan with the sauce, allowing them to cook together "to become one." The pasta absorbs some of the sauce and the sauce melds with the pasta. Add some of the reserved pasta water to loosen up the mixture. The water gives the dish a velvety touch by adding a little starch from the pasta cooking water. As it's cooking, keep checking the pasta to see if it's done. You'll want to cook the pasta "al dente," so it still has some bite to it.

*Four-Cheese Broccoli Bake, page 134*

*The Other Meatballs & Spaghetti, page 82*

*Penne with Arrabbiata Sauce, page 79*

## WHICH SAUCE GOES WITH MY PASTA?

When pairing pastas with sauces, nothing is set in stone. Play around and find the shape that fits your sauce best! We've listed three major groups of pasta. (Note the names of the pastas reflect their shapes.) Pastas within each group may be used for each other in a recipe.

### STRANDS OF PASTA

**STRANDS (SPAGHETTI FAMILY)**

*Very Thin Pasta Strands:* *Capelli d'angelo* (angel hair), *capellini* (a little thicker than angel hair), also *fedelini* or "little faithful ones"), *spaghettini* (thin long cords), *vermicelli* ("little worms," very thin), *Thicker Strands:* *Bucatini & perciatelli* (long hollow strands), *fusilli* ("little springs" or twisted spirals), *spaghetti* ("little strings"). Top with spicy tomato meat sauces or rich cream sauces.

**RIBBONS (FETTUCCINE FAMILY)**

*Egg noodles* (made with egg yolks), *fettuccine* ("little ribbon" 1/4-inch-wide flat noodles), *lasagna* (long wide strips with straight or curly edges), *lasagnette* (narrow lasagna), *linguine* ("little tongues," 1/8 inch wide), *mafalde* (wide ribbons with one ruffled edge), *pappardelle* (ribbon noodles, 1-inch wide), *tagliatelle* (a little wider than fettuccine) Try: Light tomato sauces, sauces with ricotta, butter sauces on narrow ribbons. Hearty meat ragus, vegetable and thick cream sauces on wider ones.

**ASIAN NOODLES** *Cellophane noodles* (bean threads), *Chinese-style egg noodles* (often bright yellow, made from wheat), soba (thin brownish gray noodles, made from buckwheat & wheat flours). Serve plain or with a peanut sauce.

### TUBES OF PASTA

**SMALL TUBULAR SHAPES**

*Elbows: cappelletti* ("little hats"), *cavatappi* (corkscrews), *macaroni* (*maccheroni* in Italian), *penne* ("little quills" with diagonally cut ends), *tubetti* ("little tubes"). Thick meat ragus, sauces with ricotta and/or mozzarella. Serve in: cheese sauces, salads, soups, stews.

**LARGE TUBULAR SHAPES**

*Tubes: cannelloni* ("large reeds"), *manicotti* ("small muffs" for stuffing), *mostaccioli* ("little mustaches," 2 inches long, plain or ribbed) *rigatoni* (large macaroni with grooves), *ziti* ("bridegrooms"). Match with: thick meat ragus, sauces with ricotta, sauces with mozzarella, and baked dishes.

### SPECIAL SHAPES

*Smaller: cavatelli* (shells with rippled edges), *creste di gallo* ("cockscombs" resembling a rooster's crest, *farfalle* ("butterflies," also called bow ties), *fusilli* ("little springs"), *orecchiette* ("little ears"), *radiatore* ("little radiators" with deep ribs), *ruote* ("cartwheels" with spokes), *rotini* (corkscrews), *tortellini* ("little stuffed twists). Toss into salads or with light vegetable and cream sauces, vinaigrettes, butter and cheese sauces, and light fresh tomato-basil sauces.

*Larger: Conchiglie* ("conch shells" for stuffing), *manicotti* ("small muffs" of tubes for stuffing), *ravioli* (stuffed squares). Perfect with: robust beef or pork sauces, thick sauces with mozzarella, ricotta, cream. Use in layered bakes with meat sauces and chunks of vegetables.

**SOUP PASTAS**

*Tiny shapes: alphabets* (mini letter-shaped pasta), *acini de pepe* ("peppercorns," rice shaped), *quadruci* (tiny flat squares), *orzo* (rice-shaped), *ditalini* ("tiny thimbles"), *tubetti* (little tubes), *semi de melone* ("melon seeds"), *pastina* ("tiny dough"). Toss into thin broth soups, tomato-based soups, and cream soups.

## NO-STRESS ENTERTAINING

When cooking pasta for more than a few folks, do what the restaurant chefs do and partially cook the pasta ahead of serving time. (This works only with dry pasta, not fresh.) Cook pasta about two-thirds of the normal cooking time. Drain it well and toss it with a teaspoon of olive oil to hold it without

### Cooking Basics

#### FAST WAYS TO TRANSFORM A JAR OF RED SAUCE

All these recipes work with 1 pound of pasta and one 15-ounce jar of tomato sauce. Serve with grated Parmesan cheese.

**TOMATO-MUSHROOM SAUCE** Sauté 2 cloves minced garlic, 4 ounces presliced cremini, white, or portobello mushrooms in 2 tablespoons olive oil in a large skillet until tender. Stir in one 15-ounce jar of red sauce, heat until bubbling, and serve.

**TOMATO SAUCE WITH ONIONS, PEPPERS, & SAUSAGES** Sauté 1 sliced kielbasa sausage (about 1 pound) in 2 tablespoons olive oil for 2 minutes. Stir in 1 sliced red bell pepper, and 1 chopped medium yellow onion. Cook 3 to 4 minutes more or until soft. Stir in one 15-ounce jar of red sauce, heat until bubbling, and serve.

**PALE PINK SAUCE** Heat one 15-ounce jar of red sauce until bubbling. Stir in 1/2 cup ricotta. Heat and serve.

**NIÇOISE STYLE**
Heat one 15-ounce jar of red sauce until bubbling. Stir in 1 can (7 1/2 ounces) tuna in olive oil (stir in the oil as well) and 1/2 cup diced Kalamata or oil-cured black olives.

**TOMATO & PEPPER SAUCE**
Heat one 15-ounce jar of red sauce until bubbling. Stir in 1 cup of diced roasted red pepper (the jarred ones are fine).

**DOUBLE TOMATO SAUCE**
Heat one 15-ounce jar of red sauce until bubbling. Stir in 1 cup diced sun-dried tomatoes in oil.

**HERBED TOMATO SAUCE**
Heat one 15-ounce jar of red sauce until bubbling. Stir in 1/4 cup chopped fresh herbs such as basil, mint, chives, tarragon, rosemary, parsley, or a combination.

**SMOKEY GIOVANNI'S** Heat one 15-ounce jar of red sauce until bubbling. Serve over 1 pound hot pasta and sprinkle with grated smoked mozzarella and chopped basil. Serve over *pappardelle*.

**ALL-AMERICAN MEAT SAUCE** Sauté 1 pound ground beef, veal, turkey, or a combination in 1 tablespoon of olive oil with 1 clove minced garlic and a pinch of red pepper flakes until no longer pink. Drain off any excess fat and stir in one 15-ounce jar of red sauce. Heat until bubbling and serve.

**THAT'S A SPICY SHRIMP!**
Sauté 1 pound shelled medium shrimp (tails removed) in 2 tablespoons olive oil with 1 clove minced garlic and 1/2 teaspoon red pepper flakes for about 2 minutes, or just until shrimp turn opaque. Remove shrimp with a slotted spoon, add one 15-ounce jar of red sauce to the pot, and heat until bubbling. Stir in the shrimp and heat 1 to 2 minutes more. until the shrimp are hot. Serve over pasta with chopped parsley.

**SPANISH HOLIDAY** Heat one 15-ounce jar of red sauce until bubbling and stir in 1/2 cup salsa and 1/8 teaspoon red pepper flakes. Serve over hot fusilli.

*Fettuccine Salad*, page 70

any stickiness. You can do this several hours ahead of time and refrigerate the pasta in a resealable bag, or up to 1 hour ahead and hold it at room temperature. Right before serving, finish the pasta by cooking it in the sauce—or throw it into a pot of boiling water for 1 minute to heat up. Supper's ready!

### BEST-DRESSED PASTAS

The best American and Italian pastas are made from semolina, a coarse grind of durum wheat—most from American, and Canadian wheat fields. Although both American and Italian companies make very good commercial pastas, the best pastas come from small artisan makers in Italy. (Look on the labels to find out where the pasta was made.) These artisan pastas are extruded through bronze dies and dry very slowly, creating a rough, quite porous surface. They absorb sauces very well and cook up beautifully, in the same timing (between 7 and 12 minutes) as commercially dried pastas. On the other hand, commercial pastas are extruded through Teflon dies and dried very quickly. These procedures create a slick, nonporous surface on the pasta, making it harder for the pastas to absorb sauces or for the sauce to cling.

### LEFTOVER GOLD!

Leftover pasta is a great thing to have. Toss it with a teaspoon of oil and store it in an airtight container. Cooked pasta holds from 3 to 5 days in the refrigerator. Reheat the pasta by throwing it into boiling water for a minute—or into the microwave, in a microwavable container, for 1 minute on High. Or, don't even bother to reheat the pasta and just stir it into a frittata or fry it in olive oil to make crispy noodles!

### 4 BRILLIANT NO-COOK SAUCES

No-cook sauces are one of the keys to pasta on the fast lane. Starting with freshly made pasta in the grocer's refrigerated section, you can whip up your own no-cooks in minutes!

**TWO-CHEESE SPAGHETTI POT** A winner with kids! Just combine ¼ cup each grated Pecorino Romano and Parmesan with 2 to 3 tablespoons heavy cream. Add 4 to 6 ounces cooked pasta and stir until pasta is coated.

**MARINATED FRESH TOMATOES** Chop and drain the tomatoes from a 28-ounce can of whole tomatoes. Chop a small garlic clove with ¼ teaspoon salt until the garlic becomes a purée. Stir into the tomatoes with 2 to 4 tablespoons extra-virgin olive oil and ½ teaspoon freshly ground black pepper. Toss with 8 ounces freshly cooked (hot!) pasta, some freshly grated Parmesan cheese, and a few torn basil leaves.

**BRIE VARIATION** Stir in 1 pound of Brie, rind removed, chopped into small pieces.

**ROASTED RED PEPPER SAUCE** Purée 1 jar (7 ounces) roasted red peppers with 1 clove chopped garlic, ¼ cup chopped parsley, and ½ cup fresh goat cheese. Toss with 1 pound of hot pasta.

Check out some of our favorite Pasta Perfect recipes:

**Pasta with Homemade Meat Sauce (page 25)**

**Shrimp Linguine Primavera (page 33)**

**Orange-Lemon Angel Hair Pasta, (page 43)**

**Macaroni & Three Cheeses (page 57)**

**Michael's Pasta (page 67)**

**Penne Rustica (page 78)**

**Beer Brat Pasta (page 80)**

**Snake Alley Noodles (page 91)**

**Ravioli Alfredo (page 105)**

**Pork Linguine Salad (page 111)**

**Italian Chicken Pasta (page 120)**

**Easy Classic Lasagna (page 129)**

**Beef & Mozzarella Pie (page 132)**

*Shrimp Linguine Primavera, page 33*

*Orange-Lemon Pasta, page 43*

*Beef & Mozzarella Pie, page 132*

*Tortellini with Tomatoes & Zucchini, page 24*

# Pasta Every Day

Pasta's the ultimate fast food, so naturally it's often top on the menu during busy days. Look for the recipes that use fresh pasta and cut down the pasta cooking time 75 percent. Our collection gets you in and out of the kitchen fast by using cans of vegetables for a tortellini sauce, shelled shrimp for a spaghetti topping, and a fresh lemon-butter sauce for a pasta toss. You'll find a primavera to make in a flash, a clam sauce to toss up in minutes, and the easiest Chili Mac you've ever seen. Thanks to many quick-cooking techniques and a storehouse of the right ingredients that do the work for you, you can get to the best part of enjoying a different pasta every day—the eating!

SuperQuick

# Flash Primavera

*Prep* **15 MINUTES** *Cook* **15 MINUTES**

- 1 package (16 ounces) mostaccioli (moustaches) or ziti
- 1 head broccoli or cauliflower, cut into small florets
- 1 tablespoon cornstarch
- ¼ cup water
- 1 can (14½ ounces) reduced-sodium chicken broth
- 3 garlic cloves, minced
- 1 package (10 ounces) frozen mixed vegetables
- 1 package (10 ounces) frozen chopped spinach, thawed
- Salt and pepper
- 1 cup grated Parmesan cheese

*Thaw the spinach fast in the microwave. Squeeze it well to remove all of the excess water, or the finished dish will be "soup."*

**LET'S BEGIN** Cook pasta according to package directions. Add the broccoli during the last 3 minutes of cooking. Drain pasta and broccoli and transfer to a serving bowl. Keep warm.

**SIMMER & STIR** Meanwhile, mix the cornstarch and water together in a cup until blended. Combine the broth and garlic in a large saucepan. Cook over medium heat for 3 minutes. Whisk in the cornstarch mixture until smooth.

**INTO THE PAN** Stir in the vegetables and spinach and cook for 5 minutes, or until heated through. Add to the pasta, season with salt and pepper, and add half of the Parmesan. Toss until mixed well, then sprinkle with remaining cheese.

***Makes 4 to 6 servings***

*Per serving: 618 calories, 31g protein, 106g carbohydrates, 8g fat, 4g saturated fat, 16mg cholesterol, 801mg sodium*

## Cooking Basics

### WHEN IS PASTA DONE?

The best way to know if pasta is done is to take a taste. The cooking times on the package directions are calculated from the moment water returns to a full boil after adding the pasta. If cooking fresh pasta, start testing for doneness after 30 seconds; after 7 minutes when cooking dried pasta. Fish out a piece of pasta with tongs or a long-handled fork. Let it cool slightly, then bite into it. Pasta is done when it's tender yet still slightly resistant—or *al dente*, Italian for "to the tooth." This signifies the pasta is not too soft or overdone but just right. Drain it fast, or it'll continue cooking in the hot water.

SuperQuick

# Pasta with Prosciutto & Vegetables

*Prep* **20 MINUTES** *Cook* **10 MINUTES**

- 8 ounces medium shells
- 1 tablespoon olive oil
- 2 cups sliced white mushrooms
- 1 jar (26 ounces) roasted red pepper with Italian herbs pasta sauce
- 1 can (14 ounces) artichoke hearts, drained and chopped
- 1 cup frozen green peas
- ½ cup chicken broth
- ½ cup thinly sliced prosciutto or deli ham (about 3 ounces)

Grated Parmesan cheese (optional)

*The quickest way to grate a good amount of Parmesan is in a food processor. Cut a wedge into large chunks and process it until finely chopped. Wrap and store in the refrigerator.*

**LET'S BEGIN** Cook the pasta according to package directions. Drain, transfer to a serving bowl, and keep warm.

**COOK IT QUICK** Meanwhile, heat the olive oil in a large skillet over medium-high heat. Sauté the mushrooms for 5 minutes, or until tender. Stir in the pasta sauce, artichoke hearts, peas, broth, and prosciutto. Reduce the heat and simmer for 5 minutes, or until heated through.

**SERVE** Spoon the sauce over the pasta and sprinkle with Parmesan, if desired.

***Makes 4 servings***

*Per serving: 438 calories, 19g protein, 74g carbohydrates, 8g fat, 2g saturated fat, 5mg cholesterol, 1,029mg sodium*

## Cooking Basics

### 3 QUICK STEPS TO A PERFECT POT OF PASTA

**1. Choose a large stockpot** (around 8 quarts), preferably one that's taller than it is wide. Fill it two-thirds full with fresh cool water (about 4 quarts of water for every pound of pasta). Forget the oil, as you don't need it. When there's plenty of water in the pot, the pasta won't stick together.

**2. Bring the water to a rolling boil** over high heat. If you add pasta to water that's not boiling rapidly, it'll stay longer in the cooking water and absorb too much water, making it soft and mushy. Add some salt to the cooking water before it comes to a boil. Salt not only adds flavor but ensures firm, not sticky, pasta.

**3. Add the pasta gradually** to the boiling water, not all at once, so the water continues to boil. Start timing the pasta when the water returns to a full boil. When the pasta reaches al dente (firm bite), drain pasta in a colander. Don't rinse pasta unless using it in salads or storing in the refrigerator.

*SuperQuick*

## Rigatoni in Vodka Sauce

*Prep* **15 MINUTES** *Cook* **15 MINUTES**

- 1 package (16 ounces) rigatoni or penne
- 1 tablespoon olive oil
- 1 medium onion, chopped
- 1 garlic clove, chopped
- ¼ cup vodka or chicken broth
- 1 jar (26 ounces) tomato and basil pasta sauce
- 1 jar (16 ounces) creamy Alfredo pasta sauce
- Chopped fresh basil (optional)

*Vodka has an unusual affinity for tomato. This dish has been so well received that it has become a classic in Italian restaurants.*

**LET'S BEGIN** Cook the pasta according to package directions. Drain and keep warm.

**MAKE IT SAUCY** Meanwhile, heat the oil in a medium saucepan over medium-high heat. Sauté onion for 4 minutes. Add garlic and cook for 30 seconds. Stir in vodka and cook 1 minute longer. Stir in the two pasta sauces and bring to a boil. Reduce heat to medium-low. Simmer, stirring, for 4 minutes.

**TOSS & SERVE** Toss the pasta with the sauce in a large serving bowl. Sprinkle with basil, if you wish.

***Makes 6 servings***

*Per serving: 577 calories, 13g protein, 81g carbohydrates, 19g fat, 5g saturated fat, 31mg cholesterol, 857mg sodium*

*SuperQuick*

## Lemon Pasta

*Prep* **12 MINUTES** *Cook* **15 MINUTES**

- 12 ounces linguine
- ½ cup margarine product
- ¼ cup Dijon mustard
- 2 garlic cloves, chopped
- 1 tablespoon lemon juice
- 3 tablespoons chopped fresh parsley
- Dash ground black pepper

*This is one of the most elegant, and easiest, ways to serve pasta. It makes a fabulous first course, so consider it for your next dinner party. A special addition: top with a few grilled or sautéed shrimp.*

**LET'S BEGIN** Cook the pasta according to package directions. Drain and keep warm.

**COOK IT UP** Meanwhile, melt the margarine with the remaining ingredients in a large saucepan over medium heat. Cook for 3 minutes, or until hot. Add the pasta and toss.

***Makes 4 servings***

*Per serving: 538 calories, 11g protein, 65g carbohydrates, 24g fat, 5g saturated fat, 0mg cholesterol, 619mg sodium*

SuperQuick

# Hot & Spicy Broccoli Beef

*Prep* **15 MINUTES** *Cook* **15 MINUTES**

- 12 ounces Asian noodles or linguine
- 2 tablespoons vegetable oil
- 1 pound flank steak, cut lengthwise in half, then crosswise into strips
- 3 cups broccoli florets
- ½ cup water
- ½ teaspoon garlic powder with parsley
- ½ teaspoon seasoned salt
- ½ teaspoon seasoned pepper
- ½ teaspoon red pepper flakes
- ¼ cup ketchup
- 1 to 2 tablespoons soy sauce
- ½ teaspoon ground ginger
- 1½ teaspoons cornstarch

*This great dish can be "prepped" ahead so you are ready to go at dinnertime. Cut up the steak and broccoli and refrigerate in plastic bags, then mix up the sauce and set aside.*

**LET'S BEGIN** Cook the pasta according to package directions. Drain and keep warm.

**STIR-FRY** Heat the oil in a large skillet over medium-high heat. Stir-fry the beef for 4 minutes, or just until browned. With a slotted spoon, transfer the meat to a bowl. Stir in the next 6 ingredients to the skillet. Cover and cook for 5 minutes.

**MAKE IT SAUCY** Mix the ketchup, water, soy sauce, ginger, and cornstarch in a bowl until blended. Return the meat to the pan along with the ketchup mixture. Stir-fry for 2 minutes, or until the sauce thickens and boils. Line a large platter with the pasta and top with the stir-fry mixture.

***Makes 4 servings***

*Per serving: 600 calories, 38g protein, 74g carbohydrates, 17g fat, 5g saturated fat, 46mg cholesterol, 721mg sodium*

*Rigatoni with Olives & Bacon*

SuperQuick

## RIGATONI WITH OLIVES & BACON

*Prep* **12 MINUTES** *Cook* **15 MINUTES**

- 8 ounces rigatoni or other tube shape
- 6 slices bacon
- 1 medium onion, thinly sliced
- 12 cured black olives, such as Kalamata, pitted and chopped
- Salt and ground black pepper
- Parmesan cheese shavings
- 2 tablespoons coarsely chopped marjoram or thyme (optional)

*If using Kalamata olives, buy them already pitted—less work for you!*

**LET'S BEGIN** Cook the pasta according to package directions. Drain and keep warm. Cook the bacon until crisp in a medium skillet and drain on paper towel. Chop coarsely.

**SAUTÉ IT QUICK** Sauté onion in the bacon drippings in the skillet for 5 minutes, or until just beginning to brown.

**SERVE** Transfer the pasta to a large serving bowl. Add the bacon, onion, and olives, season with salt and pepper, and toss to mix well. Top with Parmesan shavings, plus marjoram, if desired.

***Makes 4 servings***

*Per serving: 324 calories, 13g protein, 45g carbohydrates, 10g fat, 3g saturated fat, 14mg cholesterol, 541mg sodium*

SuperQuick

## PORK & PASTA SKILLET SUPPER

*Prep* **12 MINUTES** *Cook* **15 MINUTES**

- 4 ounces penne or other small tube pasta
- 1 pound ground pork
- 1 medium onion, chopped
- 1 can (14½ ounces) pasta-ready tomatoes
- 1 can (8 ounces) tomato sauce
- 1 small yellow summer squash or zucchini, thinly sliced

*Cut preparation time by substituting small broccoli florets. Or for a different flavor, add your favorite mix of wild mushrooms.*

**LET'S BEGIN** Cook the pasta according to package directions. Drain and keep warm.

**MAKE IT SAUCY** Heat a large nonstick skillet over medium-high heat. Add the pork and onion and cook for 5 minutes, or until the meat is brown.

**SIMMER LOW** Stir in the tomatoes and tomato sauce and bring to a boil. Reduce heat and simmer for 5 minutes. Stir in the squash and pasta. Cook for 2 to 5 minutes, or until hot.

***Makes 4 servings***

*Per serving: 468calories, 25g protein, 32g carbohydrates, 26g fat, 9g saturated fat, 82mg cholesterol, 952mg sodium*

SuperQuick

# Tortellini with Tomatoes & Zucchini

*Prep* **12 minutes** *Cook* **18 minutes**

*Popping the beef into the freezer for a short while (until very firm) makes it a snap to slice as thinly as you like. It is a classic Chinese technique, as so many of their dishes require thinly sliced meat.*

- 1 package (9 ounces) refrigerated cheese tortellini or ravioli
- 2 tablespoons vegetable oil
- 12 ounces boneless beef sirloin steak, cut into thin strips
- 1 medium onion, cut into thin wedges
- 1 can (14 ounces) diced tomatoes with basil, garlic, and oregano
- 1 can (14 ounces) zucchini with Italian-style tomato sauce
- Grated Romano or Parmesan cheese

**LET'S BEGIN** Cook the pasta according to package directions. Drain and keep warm.

**BROWN IT** Meanwhile, heat the oil in a large skillet over medium-high heat. Cook the beef for 5 minutes, or until brown. Using a slotted spoon, transfer the beef to a bowl.

**MAKE IT SAUCY** Add the onion to the drippings in the skillet and cook, stirring, for 3 minutes. Stir in the tomatoes with their juice and the zucchini and sauce and bring to a boil. Reduce heat and simmer, uncovered, for 6 to 8 minutes, until slightly thickened. Stir in the beef and heat through. Serve over pasta in a large serving bowl and sprinkle with cheese.

***Makes 4 servings***

*Per serving: 450 calories, 31g protein, 46g carbohydrates, 16g fat, 4g saturated fat, 88mg cholesterol, 1,242mg sodium*

## On the Menu

***A quick-to-fix hearty supper that's perfect for a cold winter's night.***

*Melon with Lime*

*Tortellini with Tomatoes & Zucchini*

*Hearts of Romaine with Cucumber & Red Wine Vinaigrette*

*Hot Garlic Twists*

*Vanilla Ice Cream with Mandarin Oranges*

SuperQuick

# Pasta with Homemade Meat Sauce

*Prep* **10 MINUTES** *Cook* **15 MINUTES**

- **12 ounces spaghetti**
- **1 pound ground beef**
- **1 can (14½ ounces) diced tomatoes with basil, garlic, and oregano**
- **1 can (8 ounces) tomato sauce**

*It used to be that making your own spaghetti sauce was a day's project. In this super recipe, just four ingredients are turned into a fresh-tasting sauce your family will love.*

**LET'S BEGIN** Cook the spaghetti according to package directions, Drain and keep warm.

**INTO THE PAN** Meanwhile, cook the beef in a large skillet over medium heat for 6 minutes, or until brown, breaking it up with a spoon. Drain off the fat. Stir in the tomatoes with their juice and the tomato sauce.

**SIMMER IT LOW** Simmer, stirring occasionally, for 15 minutes. Transfer the pasta to a large serving bowl and spoon the spaghetti sauce on top.

***Makes 4 to 6 servings***

*Per serving: 673 calories, 33g protein, 77g carbohydrates, 25g fat, 10g saturated fat, 85mg cholesterol, 957mg sodium*

# LASAGNA ROLLS

*Prep* **30 MINUTES** *Cook* **10 MINUTES** *Microwave* **12 MINUTES**

- 6 lasagna noodles
- 12 ounces ground turkey
- 1 cup ricotta cheese
- 1 cup shredded mozzarella cheese (4 ounces)
- ¼ cup grated Parmesan cheese
- ½ teaspoon Italian seasoning
- 1 can (15 ounces) Italian-style tomato sauce

*This unusual technique of stuffing and rolling up a lasagna noodle gives each guest his own individual "little lasagna." And the microwave turns it into a very fast supper dish.*

**LET'S BEGIN** Cook the noodles according to package directions. Drain and spread out on a clean kitchen towel.

**INTO THE PAN** Meanwhile, cook the turkey in a large skillet on medium-high heat for 10 minutes or until lightly browned, breaking into small pieces and stirring frequently. Add the ricotta, mozzarella, Parmesan cheese, and Italian seasoning; mix well.

**FILL & ROLL** Spread ½ cup of the turkey mixture on each lasagna noodle, then roll up tightly. Place, seam-side down, in a microwavable dish and top with the tomato sauce. Cover and microwave on High for 12 minutes, or until heated through, rotating the dish after 6 minutes.

**Makes 6 servings.**

*Per serving: 350 calories, 24g protein, 28g carbohydrates, 16 fat, 8g saturated fat, 82mg cholesterol, 649mg sodium*

SuperQuick

# QUICK CHILI MAC

*Prep* **5 MINUTES** *Cook* **22 MINUTES**

*Pick your favorite fixings to serve with this perfect weeknight dish: shredded Cheddar, sour cream, chopped red pepper, sliced scallions, or taco chips. Your choice!*

- 1 pound lean ground beef
- 1 large onion, chopped
- 1 can (14 ounces) Mexican-style stewed tomatoes
- 1½ cups water
- 3 tablespoons naturally brewed soy sauce
- 1 tablespoon chili powder
- 1½ cups small shells
- Chopped fresh cilantro or parsley

**LET'S BEGIN** Cook the beef and onion in a large skillet over medium-high heat for 5 minutes, or until brown, breaking up the beef with a spoon.

**STIR IT IN** Stir in the tomatoes, water, soy sauce, and chili powder and bring to a boil. Reduce the heat, cover the skillet, and simmer for 5 minutes. Stir in the pasta. Cover and simmer, stirring once, for 10 to 12 minutes, until the pasta is tender.

**SERVE** Sprinkle with cilantro and serve.

**Makes 6 servings**

*Per serving: 308 calories, 17g protein, 22g carbohydrates, 16g fat, 6g saturated fat, 57mg cholesterol, 691mg sodium*

## Cook to Cook

### HOW DO YOU GET GREAT FLAVOR IN PASTA DISHES?

"***I like to finish cooking pasta the last 5 minutes right in the sauce.*** This gives extra flavor to the pasta, without making it too mushy or soft. But watch it carefully. You might need to add a little liquid the last couple of minutes to keep the pot from getting too dry.

Whenever I need to add liquid to a red sauce, it never hurts to ***add a splash of a dry red wine or grape juice.*** The alcohol from the wine will bubble out of the pot, leaving a deeper complex flavor to the sauce. And the grape juice adds a nice fruity touch.

And when I make tomato sauce or meat sauce, I always double or triple the recipe. Then I freeze the extras in resealable bags (after the sauce has cooled). ***I put in a little less salt and pepper as the flavors tend to intensify in the freezer.*** When it's time to reheat the sauce, ***I thaw it in the microwave,*** then bubble it a few minutes on the range. I like to ***freshen up the pot with basil and parsley.***"

# Lone Star Steak & Pasta

*Prep* **25 MINUTES** *Cook* **15 MINUTES**

- 1 package (16 ounces) rotini or penne
- 1¼ pounds boneless beef top sirloin steak, 1 inch thick, trimmed
- 1 tablespoon olive oil
- 1 can (10 ounces) diced tomatoes with green chilies
- 1 can (16 ounces) black beans, rinsed and drained
- 1 green bell pepper, chopped
- 1 cup frozen corn, thawed and drained
- ¼ cup lime juice
- ½ cup loosely packed fresh cilantro leaves
- ¼ cup sliced scallions
- 1 clove garlic, minced
- ½ teaspoon ground cumin
- 1 teaspoon salt

*In Texas, they like their beef, and plenty of it! Here, it's simmered in a spicy tomato sauce, then spooned over spirals of hot pasta.*

**LET'S BEGIN** Cook pasta according to package directions. Drain and transfer to a platter. Meanwhile, cut steak length-wise in half, then crosswise into ⅛-inch-thick strips.

**INTO THE PAN** Heat the oil in a large nonstick skillet over medium-high heat. Add the steak, half at a time, and cook for 1 to 2 minutes per side, or until the outside surface is no longer pink. Remove the steak and set aside.

**MAKE IT SAUCY** Add the tomatoes with their juice and all of the remaining ingredients to the same skillet. Cook, stirring, for 3 minutes. Return the steak to the skillet and cook 2 minutes longer, or until heated through. Spoon over pasta.

***Makes 6 to 8 servings***

*Per serving: 582 calories, 33g protein, 77g carbohydrates, 15g fat, 5g saturated fat, 62mg cholesterol, 706mg sodium*

## Food Facts

### What's the Difference between Pasta & Noodles?

Almost every country has some form of pasta. The Germans prefer *spaetzle*; the Poles, their pierogi; the Asians, their brown *soba* noodles. In Italian, the word *pasta* means "paste." It refers to a dough made from durum wheat flour (semolina) and water or liquid.

There are two different kinds of *pasta*—macaroni and noodles. Macaroni products are made from semolina and water; noodles, from a finely ground durum flour, water, and some egg solids, by federal regulation. Without the egg, a noodle just isn't a noodle!

SuperQuick

## Easy Beef & Pasta

*Prep* **10 MINUTES** *Cook* **16 MINUTES**

- 1 pound boneless beef sirloin steak, ¾ inch thick
- 1 tablespoon vegetable oil
- 1 can (10¾ ounces) tomato soup
- ½ cup water
- 1 bag (16 ounces) frozen vegetable and pasta blend

*Busy moms, take notice: This is the perfect speedy supper. The only prep is cutting the steak into thin strips with a thin, sharp knife.*

**LET'S BEGIN** Cut the beef into very thin strips. Heat the oil in a large skillet over medium-high heat. Sauté the beef for 5 minutes, or until brown.

**STIR IT IN** Add the soup, water, and vegetable-pasta mixture and bring to a boil. Cover and cook over low heat for 5 minutes, or until heated through.

***Makes 4 servings***

*Per serving: 456 calories, 28g protein, 30g carbohydrates, 24g fat, 9g saturated fat, 84mg cholesterol, 962mg sodium*

## Spaghetti Pie

*Prep* **15 MINUTES** *Cook* **20 MINUTES**

- 4 ounces spaghettini (very thin spaghetti), broken in half
- 1 pound ground beef
- 2 tablespoons one-step beef seasoning for spaghetti meat sauce
- 1 can (15 ounces) tomato sauce
- 1 cup shredded mozzarella cheese + extra for garnishing (optional)

*Transform thin spaghetti and meat sauce into this pasta skillet pie.*

**LET'S BEGIN** Cook pasta according to package directions. Drain and keep warm. Sauté beef in a large non-stick skillet over medium-high heat for 5 minutes, or until brown. Remove meat from skillet with a slotted spoon.

**LAYER IT** Place the pasta in the skillet in an even layer and top with the meat. Mix the seasoning and the sauce and pour it over the spaghetti. Top with 1 cup mozzarella, if you wish.

**COOK & SERVE** Cover and cook on medium heat for 10 minutes or until hot. Garnish with extra mozzarella, if desired.

***Makes 6 servings***

*Per serving: 246 calories, 18g protein, 21g carbohydrates, 10g fat, 6g saturated fat, 46mg cholesterol, 875mg sodium*

# Chicken & Linguine in Creamy Tomato Sauce

*Prep* **10 MINUTES** *Cook* **30 MINUTES**

- 1 tablespoon olive oil
- 1 pound boneless, skinless chicken breast halves, cut crosswise into ½-inch-wide strips
- 1 jar (26 ounces) pasta sauce, Old World style
- 2 cups water
- 8 ounces linguine or spaghetti
- ½ cup heavy cream
- 1 tablespoon chopped fresh basil or ½ teaspoon dried basil, crumbled

*Just a little bit of cream goes a long way in this dish. To save time, slice the chicken in the morning and place in a resealable bag in the refrigerator so it's ready to go when you're ready to cook.*

**LET'S BEGIN** Heat the oil in a large skillet over medium heat. Sauté the chicken for 5 minutes, or until brown. Transfer to a bowl and keep warm.

**STIR IT IN** Add the pasta sauce and water to the skillet and bring to a boil over high heat. Stir in the uncooked linguine and return to a boil. Reduce the heat to low. Cover the skillet and simmer, stirring occasionally, for 15 minutes, or until the pasta is tender.

**MAKE IT SAUCY** Stir in the cream and basil. Return the chicken to the skillet and cook 5 minutes, or until the chicken is cooked through.

***Makes 4 servings***

*Per serving: 572 calories, 37g protein, 55g carbohydrates, 21g fat, 8g saturated fat, 107mg cholesterol, 1,301mg sodium*

## Cooking Basics

### HOW TO CHIFFONADE

Translated from the French word, chiffonade means "made of rags." In culinary circles, to chiffonade means to make thin strips or shreds of vegetables for a sauté or for a garnish.

For a fast, flavorful garnish pastas, chiffonade some fresh basil leaves. Simply stack up about 6 clean, large basil leaves (no stems, please!) on top of each other and roll them up tightly lengthwise. Then snip into very thin strips (about ⅛ inch wide) with kitchen shears. Let them fall into airy curls on top of the pasta. They add beauty and flavor!

SuperQuick

# Angel Hair with Chicken & Vegetables

*Prep* **15 MINUTES** *Cook* **12 MINUTES**

Capelli d'angelo, *also known as angel hair, aptly describes these long, extremely fine, delicate strands of pasta.*

- **4 ounces angel hair pasta**
- **1 teaspoon olive oil**
- **¼ cup chopped onion**
- **1 small garlic clove, minced**
- **1 can (14½ ounces) Italian-style tomatoes**
- **1 package (16 ounces) frozen broccoli, cauliflower, and carrots**
- **½ pound cooked chicken, cut into bite-size pieces (1½ cups)**
- **3 tablespoons grated Parmesan cheese**

**LET'S BEGIN** Cook the pasta according to package directions. Drain and keep warm. Heat the oil in a large skillet over medium heat. Sauté the onion and garlic for 3 minutes.

**STIR IT IN** Stir in the tomatoes with their juice and the frozen vegetables. Cover and cook for 5 minutes. Stir in the chicken and cook 2 to 3 minutes longer, until the vegetables are tender.

**SERVE** Pile the pasta onto a large platter and spoon the tomato-vegetable mixture into the center. Sprinkle with the Parmesan.

***Makes 6 servings***

*Per serving: 215 calories, 16g protein, 24g carbohydrates, 6g fat, 2g saturated fat, 33mg cholesterol, 396mg sodium*

*Shrimp Linguine Primavera*

SuperQuick

## Shrimp Linguine Primavera

*Prep* **12 MINUTES** *Cook* **15 MINUTES**

- 1 package (9 ounces) fresh linguine
- 2 cups frozen vegetable blend
- 1 package (10 ounces) frozen cooked, cleaned shrimp, thawed
- ¾ cup grated Parmesan cheese
- 2 garlic cloves, minced
- ¼ cup olive oil

*Fresh linguine, cleaned frozen shrimp, and frozen vegetables make it possible to get this elegant shrimp entrée on the table super fast.*

**LET'S BEGIN** Cook the pasta according to package directions—up until the last 2 minutes of cooking time.

**COOK IT QUICK** Add the vegetables to the pasta pot and cook, stirring often, until the vegetables are tender, about 2 minutes. Drain the pasta and the vegetables into a colander and drain well. Transfer to a bowl.

**TOSS & SERVE** Add the remaining ingredients and toss.

***Makes 4 servings***

*Per serving: 476 calories, 29g protein, 43g carbohydrates, 21g fat, 5g saturated fat, 166mg cholesterol, 584mg sodium*

SuperQuick

## Shrimp Robusto

*Prep* **12 MINUTES** *Cook* **15 MINUTES**

- 1 package (16 ounces) spaghetti or linguini
- 2 tablespoons olive oil
- ¼ teaspoon red pepper flakes
- 1 pound shrimp, peeled and deveined
- 1 jar (1 pound 10 ounces) sautéed onion and garlic pasta sauce

*Short on time? Save a little more time by buying previously shelled and cleaned shrimp for this recipe. Buy large or extra-large ones.*

**LET'S BEGIN** Cook the pasta according to package directions. Drain and keep warm.

**COOK IT QUICK** Meanwhile, heat the oil in a large skillet over medium-high heat. Add the pepper flakes and cook, stirring, for 1 minute. Add the shrimp and cook for 3 minutes.

**STIR IT IN** Stir in the pasta sauce. Reduce the heat and simmer, stirring occasionally, for 5 minutes. Add the pasta to the sauce and toss until well coated.

***Makes 4 servings***

*Per serving: 732 calories, 40g protein, 102g carbohydrates, 16g fat, 2g saturated fat, 172mg cholesterol, 933mg sodium*

## Easy Linguine with Red Clam Sauce

*Prep* **15 MINUTES** *Cook* **20 MINUTES**

- 8 ounces linguine or spaghetti
- 1 tablespoon olive oil
- 1 garlic clove, finely chopped
- 2 cans (10 ounces each) chopped clams, drained, ¼ cup liquid reserved
- ¼ cup dry white wine or chicken broth
- 1 jar (26 ounces) olive and sun-dried tomato pasta sauce
- ¼ teaspoon red pepper flakes
- 2 tablespoons chopped fresh parsley (optional)

*Here's a fast way to peel garlic. Place the unpeeled clove on the work surface and press down on it with the flat side of a chef's knife. The skin will pop right off. This recipe makes four side-dish servings. For a main dish, make a double batch.*

**LET'S BEGIN** Cook the pasta according to package directions. Drain and keep warm.

**STIR IT IN** Heat the oil in a large skillet over medium-high heat. Cook the garlic for 30 seconds. Stir in the clams, the reserved liquid, and the wine. Bring to a boil over high heat. Reduce the heat to medium and cook for 5 minutes, or until the liquid reduces slightly.

**MAKE IT SAUCY** Stir in the pasta sauce and pepper flakes and return to a boil. Reduce the heat and simmer, stirring occasionally, for 5 minutes. Stir in the parsley. Add the pasta to the sauce and toss until well coated.

***Makes 4 servings***

*Per serving: 586 calories, 48g protein, 62g carbohydrates, 13g fat, 2g saturated fat, 95mg cholesterol, 903mg sodium*

### Cook to Cook

#### Can I make this sauce with other seafood?

"Yes! I like to make a red shrimp sauce. ***Use 2 cups of cooked, shelled, cleaned, and coarsely chopped shrimp for the canned clams, plus*** ¼ cup tomato juice for the clam liquid. Substitute fresh chopped marjoram for the parsley.

For special occasions, I turn this recipe into Linguine with Lobster Sauce. ***Substitute 2 cups of cooked lobster meat for the clams*** and ¼ cup white cooking wine for the clam liquid. Use slivered fresh basil instead of the parsley."

# Pasta Marinara

*Prep* **15 MINUTES** *Cook* **25 MINUTES**

- 16 ounces spaghetti or linguine
- 2 cans (28 ounces each) plum tomatoes
- 3 teaspoons olive or vegetable oil
- 5 teaspoons minced garlic
- 2 cans (6 ounces each) tomato paste
- 2½ teaspoons dried oregano, crumbled
- Salt and ground black pepper
- ⅔ cup finely chopped fresh parsley

*The classic favorite—made quickly and easily from two cans of plum tomatoes and a box of spaghetti. Dinner's ready!*

**LET'S BEGIN** Cook the pasta according to package directions. Drain and keep warm. Puree the tomatoes in a blender or food processor.

**INTO THE PAN** Heat the oil in a medium saucepan over medium heat. Sauté the garlic for 15 seconds (do not let it brown). Add the pureed tomatoes, tomato paste, and oregano and season to taste with salt and pepper.

**BUBBLE & STIR** Bring the sauce to a boil, then reduce the heat and simmer for 20 minutes. Remove from the heat and stir in the parsley. Transfer the pasta to a large serving bowl and top with the sauce.

***Makes 4 servings***

*Per serving: 629 calories, 22g protein, 119g carbohydrates, 6g fat, 1g saturated fat, 0mg cholesterol, 1,607mg sodium*

*Orange-Lemon Angel Hair Pasta* *(page 43)*

# Garden Fresh & Fast

Any season's the right time for bubbling up a pot of your favorite pasta, sautéing your pick of the fresh veggies in the market in a little olive oil, and tossing them together quick and fast. Add a splash of lemon and supper's ready to rush to the table. But that's just the beginning of the fast meals you can make with pastas and fresh veggies. There's a fettuccine made with three peppers, fusilli tossed with fresh ratatouille, and a linguine sauced with fresh tomatoes and basil. Plus we've shared secrets on cooking both pasta and vegetables to the perfect doneness, without overcooking anything. These recipes make the meal—all you need is a crisp chunk of bread and fresh grapes for dessert.

# ZESTY CALIFORNIA STUFFED SHELLS

*Prep* **30 MINUTES** *Cook* **15 MINUTES**

- 40 jumbo shells
- 1/3 cup low-fat mayonnaise
- 1/4 cup soft fresh goat cheese
- 1 tablespoon lemon juice
- 3 cups cooked turkey breast, diced
- 3 scallions, minced
- 1/4 cup crystallized ginger, finely minced
- 1/4 cup carrots, finely diced
- 1/4 cup sliced almonds
- 2 medium ripe pears, diced

Salt and black pepper

Mâche (a miniature gourmet salad green) or watercress sprigs (optional)

*Turkey salad with fresh pears and veggies turn these jumbo shells into a fast, perfect summery supper. Make ahead and chill.*

**LET'S BEGIN** Cook the pasta according to package directions. Drain well. Mix the mayonnaise, cheese, and lemon juice in a small bowl until well blended. Combine the turkey and next five ingredients in a large bowl. Add the mayonnaise mixture and toss. Season with the salt and pepper.

**STUFF & SERVE** Stuff each shell with 1 to 2 tablespoons of the filling. Arrange on a platter and garnish with mâche.

***Makes 6 to 8 servings***

*Per serving: 372 calories, 24g protein, 44g carbohydrates, 9 fat, 2g saturated fat, 68mg cholesterol, 506mg sodium*

SuperQuick

# PASTA PRIMAVERA ALFREDO

*Prep* **20 MINUTES** *Cook* **6 MINUTES**

- ½ (8-ounce) package cream cheese, cubed
- ½ cup grated Parmesan cheese plus more for serving (optional)
- ½ cup butter or margarine
- ½ cup milk
- 3 cups coarsely chopped fresh vegetables
- 1 package (9 ounces) fresh fettuccine (little ribbons)

*This may be the easiest and most delicious Alfredo sauce ever. Just a small amount of cream cheese adds richness and flavor, and there will still be some cheese left for your morning toast!*

**LET'S BEGIN** Bring a large pot of salted water to a boil. Put the cream cheese, Parmesan, butter, and milk in a large saucepan. Cook, stirring occasionally, over medium-low heat for 5 minutes, or until the cream cheese is completely melted and the mixture is smooth.

**BUBBLE & STIR** Meanwhile, add the vegetables and pasta to the boiling water and cook for 3 minutes. Drain and transfer to a large serving bowl.

**TOSS IT UP** Pour the cream cheese mixture over the pasta mixture and toss gently until mixed well. Sprinkle with additional Parmesan, if you like.

***Makes 4 servings***

*Per serving: 580 calories, 16g protein, 41g carbohydrates, 40g fat, 24g saturated fat, 156mg cholesterol, 570mg sodium*

## Time Savers

### 3 WAYS TO SAVE TIME BY KEEPING THE POT BOILING

When it comes to cooking pasta, keep your eye on the pot. The water must stay at a rapid boil at all times, especially when you're adding the pasta.

**1. Add the pasta slowly**—three or four times for a pound of pasta, about 15 seconds apart. This method maintains the temperature of the pot. If the pasta is dumped in all at once, the water stops boiling for a few minutes.

**2. Add salt to the water with the pasta.** The salt raises the temperature briefly, just enough to keep the pot boiling constantly.

**3. If the boil goes away, cover the pot** just long enough to bring the water back to a full boil (usually takes about a minute). Watch closely. As soon as the water comes back to a rapid boil, take the cover off. Cook the pasta uncovered until it's done (passes the al dente test).

*Triple-Pepper Fettuccine*

SuperQuick

## TRIPLE-PEPPER FETTUCCINE

*Prep* **12 MINUTES** *Cook* **15 MINUTES**

- 1 package (12 ounces) fettuccine (little ribbons)
- 2 tablespoons margarine or butter
- 3 bell peppers: 1 green, 1 red, 1 yellow, cut into strips
- 2 garlic cloves, minced
- 1 cup chicken broth
- ½ cup spicy brown mustard

*Every supermarket carries a rainbow of bell peppers: red, yellow, orange, green, purple. A red pepper is simply a ripened green one.*

**LET'S BEGIN** Cook the pasta according to package directions. Drain and keep warm. Melt the margarine in a large skillet over medium heat and sauté the peppers and garlic for 2 minutes, or until crisp-tender. Transfer to a bowl.

**SIMMER** Whisk the broth and mustard together in the same skillet. Simmer, stirring, for 3 to 4 minutes, until slightly thickened. Return the peppers to the skillet and cook for 2 minutes, or until heated through. Toss with the pasta.

**Makes 6 to 8 servings**

*Per serving: 292 calories, 9g protein, 47g carbohydrates, 5g fat, 1g saturated fat, 0mg cholesterol, 500mg sodium*

SuperQuick

## GARDEN-FRESH PASTA

*Prep* **15 MINUTES** *Cook* **12 MINUTES**

- 12 ounces long pasta (spaghetti, fusilli, fettuccine, linguine)
- 2 tablespoons olive oil
- 1 teaspoon minced garlic
- 12 ounces cherry tomatoes, cut into quarters
- 2 tablespoons fresh basil leaves, slivered + additional for garnish
- 1 teaspoon salt
- ¼ cup Asiago or Parmesan cheese, shredded

*Pasta you way! All it takes is fresh tomatoes, some basil leaves, a little garlic, and your favorite pasta. Top it off with fresh Parmesan.*

**LET'S BEGIN** Cook the pasta according to package directions. Drain, transfer to a serving bowl, and keep warm.

**SAUTÉ IT QUICK** Meanwhile, heat the oil in a small skillet over medium-high heat. Sauté the garlic for 3 minutes, or until soft. Stir in the tomatoes, basil, and salt, until warm.

**TOSS IT UP** Add the tomato mixture and cheese to the pasta in the bowl and toss to combine. Garnish with a basil sprigs and serve immediately.

**Makes 6 servings**

*Per serving: 282 calories, 9g protein, 45g carbohydrates, 7g fat, 1g saturated fat, 4mg cholesterol, 408 mg sodium*

## On the Menu

**Fire up the grill and enjoy a barbecue, California style.**

*Magnificent Monterey Pasta*

*Grilled Lemon Chicken*

*Mesclun with Orange & Scallions & White Wine Vinaigrette*

*Hot Popovers*

*Strawberry Lemonade*

SuperQuick

# MAGNIFICENT MONTEREY PASTA

*Prep* **12 MINUTES** *Cook* **18 MINUTES**

*Use your favorite black olives in this bold-flavored pasta dish. Niçoise, Kalamata, or even California ripe olives will do the trick.*

- 1 pound penne (pens)
- 2 tablespoons olive oil
- 1 medium zucchini, cut into matchsticks
- 1 medium yellow squash, cut into matchsticks
- 1 cup thinly sliced roasted red bell peppers
- ½ cup thinly sliced red onion
- 2 tablespoons stir-fry chicken seasoning
- 2 tablespoons sliced black olives
- ½ cup grated Parmesan cheese

**LET'S BEGIN** Cook the pasta according to package directions. Drain and keep warm.

**INTO THE PAN** Heat the oil in a large skillet over medium heat. Sauté all the vegetables and the seasoning mix for 3 to 4 minutes, until crisp-tender.

**TOSS IT UP** Combine the pasta, vegetables, olives, and Parmesan together in a large pasta bowl. Toss well.

***Makes 6 servings***

*Per serving: 376 calories, 14g protein, 62g carbohydrates, 8g fat, 2g saturated fat, 5mg cholesterol, 476mg sodium*

SuperQuick

# Orange-Lemon Angel Hair Pasta

*Prep* **12 MINUTES** *Cook* **15 MINUTES**

- 1½ pounds capelli d'angelo or capellini (angel hair pasta)
- 1 pound extra-large shrimp, peeled and deveined
- 6 garlic cloves, minced
- 1 cup olive oil
- 1 cup freshly squeezed orange juice
- 1 cup fresh orange segments
- ½ cup fresh lemon segments, diced
- ½ cup fresh basil leaves, slivered
- ¼ cup freshly shredded Parmesan cheese

*Angel hair pasta, known as capelli d'angelo is the one of the finest, pastas available. Capellini is also long and thin, but not quite as fine. Both are thought to resemble the hair of angels.*

**LET'S BEGIN** Cook the pasta according to package directions. Drain, transfer to a platter, and keep warm. Grill or boil the shrimp for 3 to 4 minutes, just until opaque.

**MAKE IT SAUCY** Whisk together the garlic, oil, and orange juice. Stir in the orange and lemon segments and basil.

**TOSS & SERVE** Transfer the pasta to a warm platter and top with the shrimp. Drizzle the orange juice dressing over pasta and shrimp. Sprinkle with the Parmesan.

**Makes 4 servings**

*Per serving: 315 calories, 48g protein, 145g carbohydrates, 60g fat, 9g saturated fat, 176mg cholesterol, 275mg sodium*

# Farfalle Primavera

*Prep* **25 MINUTES** *Cook* **22 MINUTES**

- 1 pound farfalle (bowties)
- ½ teaspoon salt
- 4 large carrots, sliced
- 1 pound broccoli florets
- 1 pound cauliflower florets
- 1 medium zucchini, halved lengthwise, then sliced
- 1 medium yellow squash, halved lengthwise, then sliced
- 2 small bell peppers: 1 green and 1 red, cut into 1-inch pieces
- 8 tablespoons extra virgin olive oil
- 2 garlic cloves, minced
- 12 to 14 fresh basil leaves
- ¾ cup heavy cream
- ½ cup grated Parmesan cheese (preferably Parmigiano-Reggiano)

*To save kitchen time, purchase bags of broccoli and cauliflower florets and bagged matchstick carrot sticks, which work just as well as carrot slices here.*

**LET'S BEGIN** Cook the pasta according to package directions. Drain and keep warm. Meanwhile, half-fill a medium saucepan with water, add the salt, and bring to a boil. Set out a large bowl of ice water. Add the broccoli to the pot and blanch for 1 minute, then transfer to the ice water. Repeat with the cauliflower and carrots, blanching the cauliflower for 1 minute and the carrots for 2 minutes.

**STIR-FRY** Heat 6 tablespoons of the oil and a few pieces of the garlic in a large skillet over medium-high heat. Add the zucchini, yellow squash, and bell peppers and sauté for 4 minutes, or until lightly browned. Transfer to a bowl. Add the remaining oil and garlic to the skillet. Sauté the carrots, broccoli, and cauliflower for 2 minutes. Return the zucchini mixture to the skillet and stir in the basil. Slowly add the cream, cooking just until the mixture begins to bubble. Remove from the heat.

**TOSS IT UP** Transfer the pasta to a large serving bowl and toss with the vegetables and ¾ of the cheese. Top with the remaining cheese.

***Makes 6 servings***

*Per serving: 651 calories, 18g protein, 74g carbohydrates, 33g fat, 11g saturated fat, 46mg cholesterol, 397mg sodium*

SuperQuick

# Bowties alle Portofino

Prep **15 MINUTES** Cook **15 MINUTES**

1 pound farfalle (bow ties) or radiatore (little radiators)

1 pound medium shrimp, peeled, deveined, and cooked

12 oil-packed sun-dried tomatoes, drained and cut into strips

8 plum tomatoes, chopped

2 bunches arugula, torn into bite-size pieces

6 sprigs fresh flat-leaf parsley, coarsely chopped

½ small bunch fresh basil, leaves coarsely chopped

¼ cup olive or vegetable oil

Juice of one large lemon

Salt and ground black pepper

*In Italy, garden-fresh sauces are tossed with pastas year 'round for fast suppers. Both farfalle and radiatore are perfect for this dish as their decorative shapes hold droplets of dressing easily.*

**LET'S BEGIN** Cook the pasta according to package directions. Drain and keep warm.

**INTO THE BOWL** Meanwhile, combine the shrimp, sun-dried tomatoes, plum tomatoes, arugula, parsley, basil, in a large pasta bowl. Add the pasta and toss.

**TOSS IT UP** Drizzle on the oil and lemon juice, then season to taste with salt and pepper. Toss until mixed well.

***Makes 6 servings***

*Per serving: 620 calories, 32g protein, 92g carbohydrates, 13g fat, 2g saturated fat, 150mg cholesterol, 200mg sodium*

## Cooking Basics

### PASTAS IN DISGUISE

These may look like grains or rice, but they're really pastas! **Couscous** (KOOS-koos) is granular semolina, made from durum wheat. It's a staple of North African cuisine and is traditionally steamed and fluffed. Couscous can be flavored with almost any fruit, vegetable, meat, seafood, herb or spice. Its versatility makes couscous indispensable as a pasta to always keep on hand.

**Ditalini** (dih-tah-LEE-nee) means "little thimbles" in Italian. They are tiny, very short, straight, smooth tubes of macaroni. This versatile pasta can be used as the base of any dish. Drop it into oven bakes, stir it into soups and stews, or toss it into salads, and stir-fry it in your wok.

**Orzo** (OHR-zoh) means "barley" in Italian—but it is really isn't barley at all. Instead, orzo is tiny, rice-shaped pasta, slightly smaller than a pine nut. Top with any sauce, add to soups, or bake in a casserole. It substitutes for rice.

**Pastina** (pah-STEE-nah) is Italian for tiny dough. Pastina is made with egg and works best in light soups. Look closely—they actually come in the shape of a five-pointed star.

SuperQuick

# GRILLED TEQUILA LIME SHRIMP

*Prep* **15 MINUTES + SOAKING** *Cook* **6 MINUTES**

*Fire up the grill—it's time for a barbecue! The recipe doubles, or even triples, easily. Pile the skewers onto a large platter, scoop the pasta into a large bowl, and shower with parsley.*

- **1 pound flavored linguine or orzo**
- **1 pound large shrimp, peeled and deveined**
- **½ yellow bell pepper, cut into ½-inch pieces**
- **6 scallions, cut into 1½-inch lengths**
- **16 cherry or pear tomatoes**
- **1 cup tequila lime marinade with lime juice**
- **1 lime, cut into 8 wedges**

**LET'S BEGIN** Preheat the grill to medium-high. Soak 8 wooden skewers in hot water for at least 15 minutes. Cook the pasta according to package directions. Drain and keep warm.

**SKEWER & BASTE** Thread the shrimp, pepper, onion, and tomatoes onto the skewers. Baste generously with the tequila lime marinade.

**FIRE UP THE GRILL** Grill the skewers, turning them, for 6 to 10 minutes, until the shrimp are opaque throughout and the vegetables are tender. Line a serving platter with the pasta. Top with skewers and garnish with the lime wedges.

***Makes 4 servings***

*Per serving: 620 calories, 39g protein, 106g carbohydrates, 4g fat, 1g saturated fat, 172mg cholesterol, 1,416mg sodium*

SuperQuick

# Spaghetti & Tuna with a Touch of Lemon

*Prep* **12 MINUTES** *Cook* **15 MINUTES**

- 1 pound linguine
- 5 tablespoons olive oil
- ¾ cup soft fresh bread crumbs
- 2 cans (6 ounces each) chunk light tuna with a touch of lemon, drained
- ¾ cup chopped fresh flat-leaf parsley
- 1 large mild red onion, cut into ¼-inch dice
- 1 garlic clove mashed to a paste with 1¼ teaspoons salt
- ¼ teaspoon red pepper flakes

*Tuna is one of those great versatile ingredients, which almost everyone loves! Mild red onion is tasty and colorful, but if you like, you can use scallions, chives, or a sweet onion instead.*

**LET'S BEGIN** Cook the linguine according to package directions, reserving 1 cup of the cooking water. Drain the pasta, transfer to a large serving bowl, and keep warm.

**SAUTÉ IT QUICKLY** Meanwhile, heat 2 tablespoons of the oil in a large nonstick skillet over medium-high heat until hot but not smoking. Add the bread crumbs and cook, stirring, for 3 minutes, or until golden brown. Transfer to a plate and spread in a thin layer. Combine the remaining 3 tablespoons oil, the tuna, parsley, onion, garlic mixture, and pepper flakes and add to the bowl with the pasta.

**TOSS & SERVE** Toss the hot pasta and tuna mixture, with as much of the reserved cooking water as needed to form a sauce. Transfer to a large serving bowl and top with the bread crumbs.

***Makes 6 servings***

*Per serving: 468 calories, 24g protein, 62g carbohydrates, 13g fat, 2g saturated fat, 30mg cholesterol, 775mg sodium*

SuperQuick

# Meaty Pasta Ratatouille

*Prep* **15 MINUTES** *Cook* **15 MINUTES**

- 1 pound fusilli (little springs) or linguine (little tongues)
- 1½ tablespoons olive oil
- 1 cup diced eggplant
- 1 cup diced zucchini
- 1 cup sliced mushrooms
- 1 jar (32 ounces) pasta sauce with sausage and peppers
- ¾ cup frozen green peas
- 2 teaspoons Dijon mustard

*Ratatouille, a classic dish from the Provençal region in France, is made with eggplant, tomatoes, fresh herbs, zucchini, onions, and pepper, all of which ripen at the same time.*

**LET'S BEGIN** Cook the pasta according to package directions. Drain and keep warm.

**SAUTÉ IT QUICKLY** Meanwhile, heat the oil in a large skillet over medium-high heat. Sauté the eggplant, zucchini, and mushrooms for 6 minutes, or until tender. Stir in the meat sauce, peas, and mustard and cook for 3 minutes, or until heated through. Serve over the pasta.

***Makes 6 servings***

*Per serving: 564 calories, 16g protein, 89g carbohydrates, 16g fat, 4g saturated fat, 13mg cholesterol, 781mg sodium*

## Cooking Basics

### HERE'S HOW LONG TO COOK PASTA PERFECTLY

To get perfect pasta, start timing after putting in the pasta and after the water returns to a boil.

**Cannelloni (large reeds)**

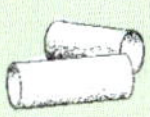

Dried 7 to 9 minutes
Fresh 2 to 3 minutes

**Capellini (little faithful ones)**

Dried 5 minutes
Fresh 5 minutes

**Farfalle (butterflies)**

Dried 7 to 10 minutes
Fresh 2 to 3 minutes

**Fettuccine (little ribbon)**

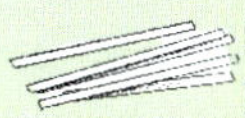

Dried 5 to 7minutes
Fresh 1 to 2 minutes

**Linguine (little tongues)**

Dried 5 to 7minutes
Fresh 1 to 2 minutes

**Ziti (bridegrooms)**

Dried 10 minutes

**Maccheroni (macaroni)**

Dried 7 to 9 minutes

**Ravioli (little turnips)**

Fresh 7 to 9 minutes

**Tortellini (little stuffed twists)**

Dried 9 to 11 minutes
Fresh 7 to 9 minutes

# PASTA WITH FRESH SALSA

*Prep* **25 MINUTES + COOLING** *Cook* **15 MINUTES**

1 pound capelli d'angelo (angel hair pasta)

2 yellow bell peppers

2 jalapeño peppers

12 to 15 plum tomatoes, chopped

1 large sweet onion, chopped

¼ cup loosely packed fresh cilantro leaves, chopped

2 tablespoons lime juice

¼ cup olive oil

Salt and ground black pepper

¼ cup grated Parmesan cheese (optional)

*Here's a way to speed up this recipe. Spoon out a jar of your favorite salsa into a bowl and combine with some fresh cilantro, lime juice, and some chopped jarred roasted red peppers.*

**LET'S BEGIN** Cook the pasta according to package directions. Drain and keep warm. Roast the bell peppers and jalapeños over an open gas burner or under the broiler until evenly charred. Place the peppers in a paper bag, seal tightly, and set aside to cool. When cool, scrape off the blackened skin, then dice the bell peppers and finely chop the jalapeños.

**FIX IT FAST** To make the salsa, combine all the roasted peppers with all the remaining ingredients except the cheese in a large serving bowl. Add the pasta and toss until mixed well. Serve with the Parmesan, if you like.

***Makes 6 to 8 servings***

*Per serving: 434 calories, 13g protein, 73g carbohydrates, 11g fat, 2g saturated fat, 0mg cholesterol, 76mg sodium*

## Cook to Cook

### SHOULD I SALT MY PASTA POT OR NOT?

"Yes, by all means, ***add salt to the pot when you're cooking pasta!*** It needs salt, and plenty of it. Pasta is such a mildly flavored food that it needs salt to bring out its very best flavors. I use at least ***1 tablespoon per pound of pasta.***

But don't worry. The pasta doesn't absorb all the salt in the water—only 10 percent is absorbed by the pasta. The rest is washed way."

SuperQuick

# Layered Picnic Pasta Salad

*Prep* **15 MINUTES** *Cook* **15 MINUTES**

- **12 ounces farfalle (bow ties) or other medium tube-shaped pasta**
- **½ cup vinaigrette salad dressing**
- **1 cup frozen green peas, thawed**
- **3 plum tomatoes, sliced**
- **1 cup sliced fresh mushrooms**
- **2 ounces prosciutto, thinly sliced**
- **2 tablespoons chopped fresh basil**
- **3 tablespoons grated Parmesan cheese**

*Tossing warm ingredients, like potatoes or pasta, with dressing is an old French trick. Warm ingredients quickly and easily absorb flavor. Try it the next time you make potato salad.*

**LET'S BEGIN** Cook the pasta according to package directions. Drain and keep warm. Return the pasta to the pot and toss with 2 tablespoons of the salad dressing.

**LAYER** Transfer half of the pasta to a clear glass bowl. Layer with the peas, tomatoes, mushrooms, and prosciutto. Top with the remaining pasta. Sprinkle with the basil and pour the remaining dressing evenly over the salad.

**SERVE IT UP** Sprinkle with the cheese and serve, or cover and refrigerate until ready to serve. (If serving later, pour remaining dressing over top just before serving.)

***Makes 6 servings***

*Per serving: 364 calories, 13g protein, 48g carbohydrates, 13g fat, 3g saturated fat, 9mg cholesterol, 332mg sodium*

## Cook to Cook

### How Long Does Pasta Keep?

"*Dried pasta stores for up to three years,* provided you keep it in its store packaging or in a tightly covered container in a cool, dry place. If pasta that is made with eggs and also egg noodles have a slightly shorter shelf life of two years.

*Fresh pasta keeps a few days in your refrigerator.* Store it in the original packaging.

*Or, pop fresh pasta into your freezer for up to three months.* Be sure to freeze it in the original, unopened packaging. For best texture, thaw in refrigerator.

I've also discovered *you can store cooked pasta, provided it doesn't have any sauce on it.* Before refrigerating, toss the pasta with a touch of oil, to prevent the pasta from sticking together. For each pound of pasta, use 1 tablespoon vegetable oil."

# Mediterranean Pasta Salad

*Prep* **12 MINUTES** *Cook* **20 MINUTES**

*A twist on the ever-popular Greek salad. The addition of pasta to this fast dish makes it hearty enough for dinner.*

- **12 ounces penne (pens) or ziti**
- **¾ pound cooked peppered pork roast, cut into thin strips**
- **1 small cucumber, peeled and diced**
- **6 ounces feta cheese, crumbled**
- **1 cup cherry tomatoes, halved**
- **½ cup chopped fresh mint**
- **½ cup Greek vinaigrette dressing**

**LETS BEGIN** Cook the pasta according to package directions. Drain and keep warm.

**TOSS AND SERVE** Gently toss all the ingredients together in a large serving bowl until mixed well. Serve in shallow salad bowls or on dinner plates.

***Makes 4 servings***

*Per serving: 420 calories, 38g protein, 27g carbohydrates, 18g fat, 10g saturated fat, 110mg cholesterol, 930mg sodium*

*Italiano Turkey Ravioli, page 65*

# Pasta & Cheese

It's a match! Pasta and cheese are simply made to go together. And our quick-cooking collection is like none other. Ham teams up with fontina in a fast penne microwave-melt, Gorgonzola and walnuts top pasta shells, and mozzarella melts into a red sauce for rotini corkscrews. Cheese is one of the best-kept secrets, and one of the most versatile ingredients, in pasta cookery. Toss fresh Parmesan with almonds and little cream right onto hot pasta to make a fast sauce. Melt Monterey Jack into a spaghetti pie one day and shred sharp Cheddar to sauce up a classic mac 'n' cheese bake another. However you slice it, shred it, melt it, grate it, or toss it, cheese and pasta make a winning dinner duo.

# Classic Mac & Cheese

*Prep* **15 MINUTES** *Cook* **35 MINUTES**

- 12 ounces elbow macaroni
- 3 tablespoons butter
- ¼ cup chopped onion
- 2 tablespoons all-purpose flour
- 2 cups milk
- 1 tablespoon mustard
- 1 2 teaspoons hot pepper sauce
- 1 teaspoon salt
- ½ teaspoon ground black pepper
- 12 ounces sharp Cheddar cheese, shredded (3 cups)
- 12 ounces coarse fresh bread crumbs (3 cups)

*Here it is—the classic recipe for mac 'n' cheese. There are lots of shredded sharp Cheddar, perfect pasta, and a crispy cheesy topping.*

**LET'S BEGIN** Preheat the oven to 375°F. Butter a 9-inch square baking dish. Cook the macaroni according to package directions. Drain, rinse, drain again, and set aside.

**MAKE IT SAUCY** Meanwhile, melt the butter in a large saucepan over medium heat. Sauté the onion for 4 minutes. Whisk in the flour and cook 1 minute. Blend the milk into the flour mixture and cook until the sauce thickens. Reduce heat to low and add the mustard, hot sauce, salt, and pepper. Stir in 2½ cups of cheese until melted. Mix in the macaroni.

**INTO THE OVEN** Pour the macaroni mixture into the baking dish. Top with remaining ½ cup cheese and bread crumbs. Bake for 25 minutes, or until top is golden brown.

***Makes 6 servings***

*Per serving: 708 calories, 29g protein, 78g carbohydrates, 31g fat, 18g saturated fat, 88mg cholesterol, 1,189mg sodium*

# Macaroni & Three Cheeses

*Prep* **12 MINUTES** *Cook* **30 MINUTES**

- 3 cups rotini or other spiral-shaped pasta (9 ounces)
- 2 tablespoons butter or margarine
- 3 tablespoons all-purpose flour
- ½ teaspoon salt
- ¼ teaspoon dry mustard
- ⅛ teaspoon ground black pepper
- ¼ teaspoon ground cayenne
- 4 cups soy milk
- 1 tablespoon cornstarch
- 1 pound shredded Cheddar and mozzarella cheese blend (4 cups)
- 6 tablespoons grated Parmesan cheese

*This extra-creamy macaroni and cheese is a great way to get your kids to enjoy soy milk! Sprinkling crushed saltine crackers or bread crumbs on top before baking adds a little crunch.*

**LET'S BEGIN** Preheat the oven to 350°F. Spray a 2-quart baking dish with nonstick cooking spray. Cook pasta according to package directions until almost tender. Drain and set aside.

**MAKE IT SAUCY** Meanwhile, melt the butter in a medium saucepan over medium heat. Stir in the flour, salt, mustard, pepper, and cayenne. Stir the soy milk and cornstarch together in a large glass measure until blended. Gradually add to the butter mixture, stirring constantly with a whisk. Bring the mixture to a boil, stirring constantly, until it thickens and bubbles. Stir in the cheese and 4 tablespoons of the Parmesan. Cook, stirring constantly, until the mixture is thick and smooth. Stir in the cooked pasta.

**INTO THE OVEN** Pour the macaroni mixture into the casserole and sprinkle with the remaining 2 tablespoons of Parmesan. Bake for 20 to 25 minutes, until the sauce bubbles.

***Makes 6 servings***

*Per serving: 590 calories, 32g protein, 41g carbohydrates, 33g fat, 20g saturated fat, 95mg cholesterol, 920mg sodium*

## Cook to Cook

### What are the fastest ways to shred cheese?

"***My food processor has a couple of shredding blades,*** just for cheese. It's of course the fastest way to shred semi-hard cheeses, such as Cheddar.

When I shred cheese by hand, ***I put the wrapped cheese into the freezer for a short time*** (30 minutes or so), just long enough to firm it up a bit.

This makes it much easier to run the cheese back and forth across the grater without it sticking or falling apart. This also helps to keep the shreds separated."

SuperQuick

# Creamy Chicken & Mushroom Fettuccine

*Prep* **12 minutes** *Cook* **15 minutes**

- 12 ounces fettuccine
- 8 ounces boneless, skinless chicken breasts, cut into ½-inch chunks
- 8 ounces mushrooms, sliced
- ½ cup chopped red bell pepper
- 1½ cups low-fat mayonnaise
- ¾ cup skim milk
- ¼ cup Parmesan cheese
- 3 tablespoons finely chopped fresh basil or 1 teaspoon dried
- 1 teaspoon coarsely ground black pepper
- ½ teaspoon paprika

*Why not use a mix of mushrooms here for the most interesting flavor and texture. These days, supermarkets carry a great variety, including white, cremini, oyster, and shiitake.*

**LET'S BEGIN** Prepare the pasta according to package directions. Drain and keep warm.

**SAUTÉ IT QUICKLY** Meanwhile, spray a large skillet with nonstick cooking spray. Sauté the chicken over medium-high heat for 4 minutes, or until golden brown and cooked through. Transfer the chicken to a bowl. Spray the skillet with cooking spray. Add the mushrooms and red pepper and sauté for 5 minutes, or until tender.

**STIR IT IN** Combine the mayonnaise, milk, cheese, basil, pepper, and paprika in a small bowl. Stir into the vegetables in the skillet, then add the chicken. Reduce the heat to medium-low and cook, stirring constantly, for 3 minutes, or until thoroughly heated.

**SERVE** Transfer the pasta to a large serving bowl and top with the chicken mixture.

**Makes 6 servings**

*Per serving: 391 calories, 20g protein, 63g carbohydrates, 6g fat, 2g saturated fat, 37mg cholesterol, 664mg sodium*

SuperQuick

# Pasta with Tomato-Gorgonzola Sauce

*Prep* **15 MINUTES** *Cook* **15 MINUTES**

- **8 ounces medium or large shells**
- **⅓ cup chopped walnuts**
- **1 jar (26 ounces) pasta sauce with roasted red peppers and Italian herbs**
- **4 ounces Gorgonzola cheese, crumbled (1 cup)**
- **¼ cup chicken broth or water**
- **½ teaspoon dried sage, crumbled (optional)**

*Toasted walnuts and gorgonzola cheese make a pasta dish that is simple yet elegant enough for company.*

**LET'S BEGIN** Cook the pasta according to package directions. Drain and keep warm. Meanwhile, toast the walnuts, tossing occasionally, in a large skillet over medium heat for 8 minutes, or until golden and fragrant.

**STIR IT IN** Add the pasta sauce, cheese, broth, and sage to the walnuts in the skillet. Cook, stirring constantly, for 5 minutes, or until the cheese melts. Transfer the pasta to a large serving bowl and top with the sauce.

***Makes 4 servings***

*Per serving: 467 calories, 18g protein, 56g carbohydrates, 19g fat, 7g saturated fat, 21mg cholesterol, 1,013mg sodium*

*Penne with Beans & Tomatoes*

SuperQuick

## Penne with Beans & Tomatoes

*Prep* **20 MINUTES** *Cook* **10 MINUTES**

- ¾ cup penne pasta
- 1 can (14½ ounces) diced tomatoes with basil, garlic and oregano
- 1 can (8 ounces) cut green beans, drained
- 1 can (8½ ounces) green lima beans, drained
- 5 ounces (about 1 cup) crumbled cooked Italian sausage
- ½ cup shredded reduced-fat mozzarella cheese

*With three cans, some sausage, and penne pasta, you can have dinner on the table in 30 minutes or less.*

**LET'S BEGIN** Cook the pasta according to package directions. Drain and keep warm.

**BUBBLE & STIR** Meanwhile, combine the tomatoes with their juice, and the drained green beans, and lima beans in a large skillet and bring to a boil. Stir in the sausage and pasta and cook until heated through. Sprinkle with the cheese.

***Makes 2 servings***

*Per serving: 573 calories, 33g protein, 60g carbohydrates, 23g fat, 9g saturated fat, 67mg cholesterol, 2,543mg sodium*

SuperQuick

## Pasta Primavera with Lemon-Pepper Sauce

*Prep* **15 MINUTES** *Cook* **15 MINUTES**

- 1 8 ounces linguine
- 1 bag (16 ounces) frozen farm fresh broccoli, cauliflower, and carrots
- 1 packet (1.8 ounces) white sauce mix
- 2 teaspoons grated lemon zest
- ¼ cup grated Parmesan cheese plus more for serving
- ¼ teaspoon cracked black pepper

*Pasta primavera is classically made with the first fresh vegetables of spring. Cut out the chopping time by using frozen vegetables.*

**LET'S BEGIN** Cook the pasta according to package directions, adding the vegetables during the last 8 minutes of cooking. Transfer to a colander and drain, then keep warm.

**STIR IT IN** Prepare the sauce mix in the same pot according to packet directions, stirring in the lemon zest, cheese, and pepper. Add the pasta and vegetables and cook over medium heat for 4 minutes, or until heated through. Serve with some cheese on the side if you wish.

***Makes 4 servings***

*Per serving: 416 calories, 17g protein, 67g carbohydrates, 9g fat, 4g saturated fat, 23mg cholesterol, 1,246mg sodium*

SuperQuick

# HAY & STRAW

*Prep* **15 MINUTES** *Cook* **15 MINUTES**

*In Italy, pasta dishes made with both plain and green (spinach) pasta are referred to as* paglia e fieno *or hay and straw. Arugula has a pleasant, peppery flavor that goes well with the goat cheese.*

- **12 ounces green and white fettuccine**
- **2 teaspoons olive oil**
- **½ cup finely chopped shallots or onion**
- **3 garlic cloves, minced**
- **¼ teaspoon red pepper flakes**
- **1 jar (7 ounces) roasted red peppers, drained, and cut into thin strips**
- **3 cups loosely packed arugula, coarsely chopped**
- **½ teaspoon dried basil**
- **¼ cup finely chopped fresh parsley**
- **½ cup mild goat cheese, crumbled (optional)**

**LET'S BEGIN** Cook the pasta according to package directions. Drain and keep warm.

**SAUTÉ IT QUICKLY** Meanwhile, heat the oil in a large saucepan over medium heat. Sauté the shallots, garlic, and pepper flakes for 2 minutes. Add the roasted peppers and sauté for 5 minutes. Add the arugula, basil, and parsley and sauté 2 minutes longer, or until the arugula wilts.

**MAKE IT SAUCY** Transfer the pasta to a large serving bowl. Pour the sauce over the pasta and toss lightly. Top with the goat cheese, if you like, and gently toss to mix.

***Makes 4 to 6 servings***

*Per serving: 371 calories, 12g protein, 71g carbohydrates, 4g fat, 1g saturated fat, 0mg cholesterol, 22mg sodium*

## On the Menu

***Make Friday pasta night and invite friends for a leisurely late supper, as in Rome.***

*Roasted Antipasto Vegetables*

*Hay & Straw*

*Grilled Beef Filet & Onions on Focaccia*

*Crenshaw Melon*
*Fresh Raspberries*

*Sparkling Water*

SuperQuick

# 2-Step Cheesy Garlic Twists

*Prep* **12 MINUTES** *Cook* **16 MINUTES**

- 8 ounces rotini pasta (corkscrews)
- 1 jar (28 ounces) traditional pasta sauce
- 4 ounces shredded mozzarella cheese (1 cup)
- ½ cup roasted garlic croutons, crushed

*If you prefer to shred your own mozzarella cheese, pop the cheese into the freezer for about 30 minutes to firm it up a bit.*

**LET'S BEGIN** Cook the pasta according to package directions. Drain and transfer to a skillet.

**COMBINE IT** Add the sauce to the pasta and heat through. Top with the cheese and sprinkle with the croutons. Cover and heat until cheese melts and pasta is hot.

***Makes 4 servings***

*Per serving: 545 calories, 18g protein, 85g carbohydrates, 15g fat, 6g saturated fat, 15mg cholesterol, 1,265mg sodium*

# Southwestern Spaghetti Pie

*Prep* **15 MINUTES** *Cook/Bake* **20 MINUTES + STANDING**

- 8 ounces spaghetti or linguine
- 8 ounces ground pork
- 1 cup chopped onion
- 1 medium green bell pepper, chopped
- 1 large garlic clove, minced
- 1 jalapeño pepper, seeded and minced
- 1 tablespoon chili powder
- ½ teaspoon ground cumin
- ½ teaspoon dried oregano
- Salt and pepper
- ½ cup skim milk
- 1 large egg
- 1 can (16 ounces) low-sodium tomato sauce
- 8 ounces shredded Monterey Jack or Cheddar cheese (2 cups)

*Here's a great twist on the classic Italian dish—pasta pie. Start the meal with a bowl of guacamole and chips and end with key lime pie, topped with swirls of whipped cream.*

**LET'S BEGIN** Preheat the oven to 425°F. Spray a 12 × 9-inch baking dish with nonstick cooking spray. Prepare the pasta according to package directions. Drain and keep warm.

**SAUTÉ IT QUICKLY** Meanwhile, sauté the pork, onion, green pepper, garlic, and jalapeño in a large skillet over medium heat for 6 minutes, or until the pork is no longer pink. Drain off the fat. Add the chili powder, cumin, oregano, salt, and pepper to the pork and cook for 2 minutes more.

**INTO THE OVEN** Whisk the milk and egg together in a small bowl, stir into the hot pasta, then pour into the baking dish. Spread the meat mixture evenly over the pasta and sprinkle cheese on top. Bake in the lower third of the oven for 10 minutes, or until the cheese has melted and the casserole bubbles. Let stand 5 minutes before serving.

***Makes 4 to 6 servings***

*Per serving: 660 calories, 36g protein, 57g carbohydrates, 32g fat, 16g saturated fat, 144mg cholesterol, 485mg sodium*

# Italiano Turkey Ravioli

*Prep* **12 MINUTES** *Cook* **25 MINUTES**

- 1 tablespoon vegetable oil
- 1 package (16 ounces) seasoned sweet or hot Italian-style lean turkey sausage, cut into ½-inch-thick slices
- 2 cups chunky-style pasta sauce
- ⅓ cup water
- 1 package (9 ounces) fresh or frozen cheese ravioli, thawed
- 1 package (10 ounces) frozen chopped spinach, thawed, drained, and squeezed dry
- 1 container (15 ounces) ricotta cheese
- ¼ cup grated Parmesan cheese
- 1 large egg, beaten

*If using frozen ravioli, be sure to put it in the refrigerator in the morning so it is nicely thawed by the time you get around to supper.*

**LET'S BEGIN** Heat the oil in a large skillet over medium-high heat. Add the sausage and cook for 8 minutes, or until cooked through. Transfer to paper towels to drain.

**BUBBLE & STIR** Add the pasta sauce and water to the skillet and bring to a boil. Stir in the ravioli. Reduce the heat to medium and cover the skillet. Cook for 3 minutes. Return the sausage to the pan.

**MAKE IT SAUCY** Combine the spinach, ricotta, Parmesan, and egg in a bowl. Add the ricotta mixture to the ravioli. Cover and cook over medium-low for 10 minutes, or until the ricotta layer is set and the ravioli is tender.

***Makes 4 to 6 servings***

*Per serving: 784 calories, 50g protein, 51g carbohydrates, 45g fat, 19g saturated fat, 222mg cholesterol, 1,854mg sodium*

## Cooking Basics

### HOW MUCH PASTA TO COOK

Although most pasta manufacturers recommend cooking 2 or 3 ounces of pasta for a main-dish serving, 4 ounces of dried or 3 ounces of fresh pasta is a more generous serving. Count on cooking a pound for four servings, depending on how hungry the crowd is. The shape also makes a difference. Tube pastas, such as ziti or rigatoni, produce more cups of pasta after cooking than strand pasta. For example, 4 ounces of egg noodles gives you 3 cups after cooking; 4 ounces of ziti, 2½ cups; 4 ounces of spaghetti or macaroni, only 2 cups.

*Michael's Pasta*

*SuperQuick*

# Michael's Pasta

*Prep* **12 MINUTES** *Cook* **15 MINUTES**

- 8 ounces radiatore or other fancy shaped pasta
- ½ cup olive oil
- 2 tablespoons lemon juice
- ¾ teaspoon garlic salt
- ½ teaspoon lemon pepper
- 3 cups chopped plum tomatoes (about 6)
- ¾ cup chopped fresh basil
- ¼ cup grated Parmesan cheese

*Plum (roma) tomatoes are meaty, meaning they are not as soft or as juicy as regular tomatoes. Great for marinated tomato salads!*

**LET'S BEGIN** Cook the pasta according to package directions, omitting the salt. Drain and keep warm

**COMBINE** Meanwhile, combine the oil, lemon juice, garlic salt, and pepper in a jar, cover tightly, and shake to mix.

**TOSS IT UP** Toss the pasta, tomatoes, basil, and oil mixture in a large bowl until mixed. Sprinkle with the cheese.

***Makes 4 servings***

*Per serving: 505 calories, 11g protein, 50g carbohydrates, 30g fat, 5g saturated fat, 4mg cholesterol, 330mg sodium*

*SuperQuick*

# California Almond Fettuccine

*Prep* **12 MINUTES** *Cook* **5 MINUTES**

- 8 ounces fettuccine or very thin egg noodles
- ¼ cup butter or margarine
- 1 cup grated Parmesan cheese
- ¾ cup blanched slivered almonds, toasted
- ½ cup heavy cream, whipped
- 2 tablespoons sliced scallions
- Salt and pepper (optional)

*Did you know that noodles are made from durum flour, water, and egg, while macaroni (pasta) is made from semolina flour and water? The addition of egg makes the noodles more delicate.*

**LET'S BEGIN** Cook the noodles according to package directions. Drain and keep warm.

**COOK IT QUICK** Meanwhile, melt the butter in the same pan over medium-low heat, then stir in the noodles. Cook, stirring, for 2 minutes, or until heated through. Add the remaining ingredients and toss gently to mix.

***Makes 4 servings***

*Per serving: 678 calories, 23g protein, 48g carbohydrates, 45g fat, 20g saturated fat, 144mg cholesterol, 528mg sodium*

# Baked Penne & Ham

*Prep* **15 minutes** *Cook* **28 minutes** *Microwave* **8 minutes**

- 2 cups penne
- 1 package (1.8 ounces) white-sauce mix
- 2 cups milk
- 1½ cups shredded fontina cheese
- 2 cups canned fried onions
- 1 cup diced boiled ham
- ⅓ cup chopped oil-packed sun-dried tomatoes, drained
- ½ cup frozen peas

*If you like, you can use Canadian bacon or smoked pork loin chops (found next to the bacon) instead of boiled ham for a slighter bolder flavor.*

**LET'S BEGIN** Cook the pasta according to package directions. Drain and keep warm. Prepare the white sauce mix according to package directions with the 2 cups milk. Stir in 1 cup of the cheese and cook over low heat, stirring constantly, until the cheese melts.

**STIR IT IN** Combine the pasta, 1 cup of the fried onions, the ham, tomatoes, and peas in a large bowl. Add the cheese sauce and toss until evenly coated. Transfer the mixture to a shallow 2-quart microwavable dish. Cover with a piece of vented plastic.

**COOK IT QUICK** Microwave on High for 5 minutes, then stir. Sprinkle with the remaining 1 cup fried onions and the remaining ½ cup cheese. Microwave on High for 3 minutes, or until the onions are golden and the cheese has melted.

***Makes 4 servings***

*Per serving: 715 calories, 30g protein, 59g carbohydrates, 38 fat, 17g saturated fat, 90mg cholesterol, 2,000mg sodium*

SuperQuick

# Fettuccine with Shrimp & Vegetables

*Prep* **12 MINUTES** *Cook* **15 MINUTES**

- 1 package (9 ounces) fresh fettuccine
- 1 cup heavy cream
- 1 cup sour cream
- 4 tablespoons butter
- 1 garlic clove, minced
- ¼ teaspoon dried sage
- ¼ teaspoon dried basil
- ¼ teaspoon dried thyme
- 1½ cup grated Parmesan cheese plus more for serving
- 1 package (16 ounces) frozen broccoli, red peppers, onions & mushrooms, thawed and drained
- 1 pound cooked, cleaned shrimp

Salt and ground white pepper

*Once you've tasted this dish, you'll want to serve it time and again. Since the sauce is so rich and creamy, 9 ounces of fresh linguine serves four, instead of the usual three—or six as a side dish.*

**LET'S BEGIN** Cook the pasta according to package directions. Drain and keep warm. Beat the heavy cream and sour cream in a small bowl with an electric mixer until thick, then set aside.

**STIR IT IN** Melt the butter in a large saucepot or deep skillet over medium-high heat. Add the garlic and sauté for 2 minutes. Reduce the heat to medium and stir in the cream mixture, sage, basil, and thyme. Simmer for 1 minute, then stir in 1 cup of the cheese.

**TOSS & SERVE** Add the pasta, vegetables, and shrimp and toss until evenly coated. Season with salt and pepper. Serve with additional cheese on the side.

***Makes 4 to 6 servings***

*Per serving: 928 calories, 50g protein, 51g carbohydrates, 59g fat, 35g saturated fat, 383mg cholesterol, 1,377mg sodium*

# Fettuccine Salad

*Prep* **12 MINUTES + CHILLING** *Cook* **25 MINUTES**

- 1 package (8 ounces) fettuccini
- ½ cup olive oil
- ⅓ cup grated Parmesan cheese
- 5 teaspoons Dijon mustard
- ¼ cup lime juice
- ¾ teaspoon seasoned pepper
- ¾ teaspoon dried basil, crumbled
- ½ teaspoon seasoned salt
- ½ teaspoon garlic powder with parsley
- 1 can (2¼ ounces) sliced black olives, drained
- 1 zucchini, sliced
- 1 tomato, chopped

*When making a pasta salad, it is always a good idea to lightly dress the pasta with a bit of oil, which prevents it from sticking together, especially if the salad sits out for a while.*

**LET'S BEGIN** Cook the pasta according to package directions. Drain and keep warm. Combine the next eight ingredients in a small bowl.

**TOSS IT UP** Transfer the pasta to a large serving bowl. Add the remaining ingredients and the dressing, tossing to mix well.

**LET IT CHILL** Cover and refrigerate for at least 1 hour or up to 4 hours before serving.

***Makes 4 servings***

*Per serving: 523 calories, 11g protein, 49g carbohydrates, 32g fat, 5g saturated fat, 5mg cholesterol, 604mg sodium*

## Cooking Basics

### STOP THE RINSE CYCLE!

Most Italians would be horrified to see anyone rinse pasta after it has been cooked. Why? Because rinsing washes away some of the pasta's outer starch, which is what helps the sauce adhere to the pasta.

But even the Italians would agree that rinsing the fettuccine for this salad is just fine. Put the hot pasta in a colander and let cold water from the faucet run through it. It rinses off any excess starch and stops the cooking at the same time. The only other time you should run pasta under the faucet is when making baked pastas.

After rinsing, if you're not saucing and serving the pasta right away, just toss it with a bit of olive oil to prevent sticking.

*Pork & Noodle Stir-fry, page 89*

# Melting Pot

Here's a way to bring your favorite little Italian ristorante home—bubble up a pot of penne pasta and a creamy rustica sauce. Toss it up, shower with Parmesan, and supper's ready. Or try sizzling some fresh shrimp for topping hot linguine, just as it's served along the Mediterranean seacoast. Then mix up a noodle stroganoff dish, toss up some sesame noodles as they do in the Orient, and stir up a vegetable stir-fry in a peanut sauce to serve over hot pasta. We've also added a down-home chicken spaghetti from the Southwest, too, and a stroganoff in true style of Russian nobility. All this and a few more pasta cooking-basics, too. Happy traveling!

SuperQuick

# SEASIDE SHRIMP LINGUINE

*Prep* **15 MINUTES** *Cook* **15 MINUTES**

- 8 ounces linguine
- 2 tablespoons butter
- 8 ounces sliced mushrooms
- 1 garlic clove, finely chopped
- ½ teaspoon lemon pepper
- ½ cup sliced scallions
- ½ pound medium shrimp, peeled and deveined
- ¼ cup half-and-half
- ¼ cup chicken broth
- 1 tablespoon cornstarch
- ½ teaspoon salt
- 2 medium tomatoes, seeded and chopped
- 1 tablespoon chopped fresh parsley

*Pasta and seafood are classic go-togethers. Here, a light sauce of fresh tomatoes, mushrooms, and garlic with a touch of lemon pepper makes this recipe a keeper.*

**LET'S BEGIN** Cook the pasta according to package directions. Drain, transfer to a serving bowl, and keep warm.

**SAUTÉ IT QUICKLY** Meanwhile, melt the butter in a large skillet over medium-high heat until sizzling. Sauté the mushrooms, garlic, and lemon pepper for 4 to 5 minutes, until the vegetables are soft. Add the scallions and shrimp, and cook for 1 to 2 minutes, until the shrimp are opaque throughout.

**MAKE IT SAUCY** Combine the half-and-half, broth, cornstarch, and salt in a small bowl and stir until blended. Add to the skillet and cook for 1 to 2 minutes, until the mixture thickens. Add the tomatoes and cook for 1 minute longer. Spoon over pasta and sprinkle with the parsley.

***Makes 6 servings***

*Per serving: 260 calories, 15g protein, 35g carbohydrates, 7g fat, 4g saturated fat, 72mg cholesterol, 417mg sodium*

## Time Savers

### PREVENT MESSY BOIL-OVERS

Let's face it: when the pasta pot boils over, you have to spend time cleaning up the mess. So by keeping the water in the pot, you'll save cleanup time later.

Here's a tip that works: Dab a little cooking oil on your finger and run it around the rim of the pot (before it starts to get hot). After you add pasta to the pot and it starts cooking, water might bubble up near the edge. If that happens, the oil on the rim will coat the water bubbles as they rise and cause them to burst—before they rise out of the pot. This means no boil-overs and no mess to clean up.

SuperQuick

# Orzo with Cranberries & Sausage

*Prep* **8 MINUTES** *Cook* **20 MINUTES**

- ½ pound sweet Italian sausage links
- 1 small onion chopped
- 12 ounces orzo, acine de pepe (peppercorns), or ditalini (thimbles)
- 3½ cups reduced-sodium chicken broth
- 1½ cups orange juice
- ½ cup dried cranberries
- ½ teaspoon dried sage

*Here's the ideal recipe for a quick autumn dinner. Sweetened dried cranberries, readily available in supermarkets in the fall, add just the right sweet-tart flavor—and are a beautiful red.*

**LET'S BEGIN** Spray a large skillet with nonstick cooking spray and set over medium heat. Cook the sausage and onion, stirring frequently, for 5 minutes, or until browned. Transfer the sausage to paper towels to drain, then chop.

**STIR IT IN** Return the sausage to the onion in the skillet. Add all of the remaining ingredients and bring to a boil, stirring occasionally. Reduce the heat and cover the pan.

**SIMMER LOW** Simmer for 15 minutes, or until most of the liquid is absorbed. Remove from the heat and let stand for 10 minutes. Toss and serve.

**Makes 8 servings**

*Per serving: 341 calories, 11g protein, 45g carbohydrates, 13g fat, 5g saturated fat, 21mg cholesterol, 254mg sodium*

SuperQuick

# Southwestern Chicken Spaghetti

*Prep* **15 MINUTES** *Cook* **15 MINUTES**

- 12 ounces spaghetti
- 1 package (1¼ ounces) spaghetti sauce mix
- 1¾ cups water
- 1 can (6 ounces) tomato paste
- 1 pound boneless, skinless chicken breast halves
- 1 can (15 ounces) black beans
- 1 tablespoon vegetable oil
- 1½ cups frozen whole kernel corn
- 2 cans (4 ounces each) diced mild green chilies
- 1 teaspoon ground cumin
- ⅛ teaspoon cayenne (optional)
- 2 tablespoons chopped fresh cilantro (optional)

*Here are many of the flavors of the Southwest, all mixed together in a chicken spaghetti supper. Quick to fix and great to eat.*

**LET'S BEGIN** Cook the pasta according to package directions. Drain and keep warm. Prepare the spaghetti sauce mix with the water and tomato paste according to package directions. Keep warm in saucepan. Cut the chicken into strips, ½-inch thick. Rinse and drain the beans.

**STIR-FRY** Meanwhile, heat the oil in a large skillet over medium-high heat. Stir-fry the chicken over medium high heat for 6 minutes, or until cooked through, then transfer to the spaghetti sauce. Stir in the beans, corn, chilies, cumin, and cayenne, if using, and cook over medium heat for 5 minutes, or until heated through.

**SERVE IT UP** Transfer pasta to a large serving bowl and top with chicken mixture. Sprinkle with cilantro, if you like.

***Makes 6 servings***

*Per serving: 443 calories, 30g protein, 72g carbohydrates, 4g fat, 1g saturated fat, 42mg cholesterol, 747mg sodium*

SuperQuick

## Penne Rustica

*Prep* **12 MINUTES** *Cook* **15 MINUTES**

- 16 ounces penne pasta
- 1 tablespoon olive oil
- ⅓ cup chopped onion
- 1 garlic clove, minced
- ¼ cup chopped drained oil-packed sun-dried tomatoes
- ¼ cup dry white wine or chicken broth
- 1 jar (16 ounces) creamy Alfredo pasta sauce
- ⅛ teaspoon ground pepper

Rustica *refers to hearty country dishes that are tasty and satisfying-not fussy. Store-bought Alfredo sauce works—one, two, three!*

**LET'S BEGIN** Cook the pasta according to package directions. Drain and keep warm. Heat oil in a large nonstick skillet over medium-high heat. Sauté the onion for 4 minutes, then add garlic and cook 30 seconds. Stir in tomatoes and wine. Bring to a boil , then stir in pasta sauce and pepper.

**BUBBLE & STIR** Reduce heat and simmer for 2 minutes. Toss with pasta and top with Parmesan shavings, if you like.

***Makes 6 servings***

*Per serving: 458 calories, 11g protein, 62g carbohydrates, 17g fat, 5g saturated fat, 31mg cholesterol, 440mg sodium*

SuperQuick

## Bowties with Vegetables Alfredo

*Prep* **20 MINUTES** *Cook* **5 MINUTES**

- 8 ounces farfalle (bowties)
- 1 bag (16 ounces) frozen farm-fresh broccoli, cauliflower and carrots mix
- 1 packet (1.6 ounces) Alfredo pasta-sauce mix
- 1 cup milk
- ½ cup water
- 1 tablespoon butter
- ½ teaspoon ground black pepper
- Grated Parmesan cheese (optional)

*They'll never know you didn't prepare the Alfredo sauce from scratch, and don't tell!*

**LET'S BEGIN** Cook the pasta according to package directions. Add the vegetables during the last 5 minutes of cooking Drain and return to the pot.

**STIR IT IN** Meanwhile, prepare the Alfredo sauce according to package directions in a medium saucepan with the milk, water, and butter. Stir the sauce into the vegetables and pasta.

**TOSS & SERVE** Cook, stirring, over medium heat for 4 minutes, or until heated through. Add the pepper and sprinkle with the Parmesan, if using, and toss again.

***Makes 4 servings***

*Per serving: 377 calories, 14g protein, 58g carbohydrates, 10g fat, 5g saturated fat, 29mg cholesterol, 903mg sodium*

SuperQuick

# PENNE WITH ARRABBIATA SAUCE

*Prep* **15 MINUTES** *Cook* **15 MINUTES**

- 24 ounces penne (pens)
- 2 tablespoons olive oil
- 8 garlic cloves
- 1 can (28 ounces) crushed tomatoes in purée
- ¼ cup chopped oil-packed sun-dried tomatoes
- 3 tablespoons cayenne pepper sauce
- 8 Kalamata olives, pitted and chopped
- 6 fresh basil leaves
- 1 tablespoon capers

*In Italian the word* arrabbiata *means "angry," which refers to the heat in this full-flavored dish. This one has hot pepper sauce.*

**LET'S BEGIN** Cook the pasta according to package directions. Drain and keep warm. Meanwhile, heat the oil in large nonstick skillet over medium heat. Sauté the garlic for 4 minutes. Add all the remaining ingredients. Bring to a boil.

**SIMMER LOW** Reduce the heat and partially cover the pan. Simmer, stirring occasionally, for 10 minutes. Toss the pasta with half of the sauce mixture in the pasta pot. Transfer to a large serving bowl and spoon the remaining sauce on top.

***Makes 8 servings***

*Per serving: 383 calories, 12g protein, 70g carbohydrates, 6g fat, 1g saturated fat, 0mg cholesterol, 377mg sodium*

# Beer Brat Pasta

*Prep* **15 MINUTES** *Cook/Bake* **25 MINUTES**

- 1 pound rigatoni or other tube-shaped pasta
- 2 red bell peppers, coarsely chopped
- 1 large onion, coarsely chopped (1 cup)
- 4 garlic cloves, minced
- 1 tablespoon olive oil
- 1 pound bratwurst, casings removed
- ½ cup beer
- ½ cup chopped fresh basil
- 1½ cups low-fat Cheddar cheese

*Your first taste will have you thinking you just stepped into a German beer hall! Make this fast dish for your next superbowl party. Save time and use pre-shredded cheese.*

**LET'S BEGIN** Preheat the oven to 425°F. Cook pasta per package directions. Drain, reserving ½ cup pasta water.

**INTO THE OVEN** Toss the red pepper, onion, garlic and oil together in a 13 × 9-inch baking dish and roast, stirring occasionally, for 25 minutes. Meanwhile, cook the bratwurst in a large skillet over medium heat for 8 minutes, or until well browned. Drain off the fat, pour in the beer, and simmer over low heat for 5 minutes.

**MIX IT UP** Add the bratwurst, pasta, basil, and 1 cup of the cheese to the vegetables and toss to mix, adding a little of the pasta water if mixture seems dry. Sprinkle with the remaining cheese.

***Makes 10 to 12 servings***

*Per serving: 383 calories, 20g protein, 39g carbohydrates, 16g fat, 7g saturated fat, 33mg cholesterol, 505mg sodium*

*SuperQuick*

# Tuscan Pasta

*Prep* **12 MINUTES** *Cook* **15 MINUTES**

*Cannellini beans are simply white kidney beans. If there is another bean you prefer to use, go for it.*

- **2 cups (8 ounces) elbow macaroni**
- **2 tablespoons olive oil**
- **½ cup coarsely chopped carrot**
- **½ cup sliced celery**
- **1 jar (26 ounces) pasta sauce with sautéed onion and garlic**
- **¼ to ½ teaspoon red pepper flakes**
- **1 can (19 ounces) cannellini or red kidney beans, rinsed and drained**
- **Chopped fresh parsley (optional)**

**LET'S BEGIN** Cook the macaroni according to package directions. Drain and keep warm.

**INTO THE PAN** Meanwhile, heat the oil in a large skillet over medium heat. Sauté the carrot and celery for 4 minutes, or until crisp-tender. Stir in the pasta sauce and pepper flakes and bring to a boil.

**SIMMER LOW** Reduce the heat to low. Cover and simmer for 5 minutes, then add the beans and cook 3 minutes longer, or until heated through. Transfer the macaroni into a serving bowl and spoon the pasta sauce on top. Garnish with parsley, if you wish.

***Makes 4 servings***

*Per serving: 566 calories, 20g protein, 90g carbohydrates, 14g fat, 2g saturated fat, 0mg cholesterol, 786mg sodium*

## *On the Menu*

***In Tuscany, the Italians like their suppers simple, hearty, & bursting with flavor.***

*Tuscan Pasta*

*Broccoli Florets with Cheese 'n' Breadcrumbs*

*Hot Baguette Rolls*

*Orange Flan & Fresh Blueberries*

*Espresso*

# THE OTHER MEATBALLS & SPAGHETTI

*Prep* **15 MINUTES** *Cook* **15 MINUTES**

- **12 ounces fusilli (little springs) or spaghetti**
- **1 pound ground pork**
- **4 tablespoons dry bread crumbs**
- **1 large egg**
- **1 tablespoon finely minced onion**
- **¼ teaspoon salt**
- **Dash hot pepper sauce**
- **1 jar (28 ounces) marinara sauce**

Here's one of the best, fastest meatball mix around, made from only six ingredients. Make a double batch and freeze them.

**LET'S BEGIN** Cook the pasta according to package directions. Drain and keep warm.

**SHAPE & SIMMER** Mix together pork, bread crumbs, egg, onion, and seasonings. Shape meat mixture into ¾-inch balls. Brown meatballs in a large skillet over medium-high heat. Remove from pan and drain off fat. Heat sauce in same skillet. Return meatballs to skillet. Cover and simmer for 10 to 12 minutes. Serve over hot pasta.

***Makes 6 servings***

*Per serving: 516 calories, 24g protein, 57g carbohydrates, 21g fat, 7g saturated fat, 90mg cholesterol, 738mg sodium*

SuperQuick

# SHRIMP DIVINE PIEROGIES

*Prep* **10 MINUTES** *Cook* **15 MINUTES**

- 1 package (16.9 ounces) potato and Cheddar cheese pierogies (frozen)
- 12 ounces medium shrimp in shells
- 1 tablespoon olive oil
- ⅓ cup pine nuts
- 2 garlic cloves, minced
- 1 can (14¾ ounces) Italian-style stewed tomatoes

*Pierogies, one of Poland's most beloved foods, are tender dumplings stuffed with a variety of fillings such as potato, cabbage, or farmer cheese.*

**LET'S BEGIN** Bring a large saucepan of water to a boil. Add the pierogies. Cook over medium heat for 5 minutes, or until thawed. Drain, transfer to serving bowl, and keep warm.

**BUBBLE & BOIL** Cook shrimp in boiling water for 1 minute, or until shrimp are pink and opaque throughout. Drain, cool under running cold water, then peel and set aside.

**SAUTÉ IT QUICKLY** Heat the oil in large skillet over medium heat. Sauté the pine nuts and garlic for 1 minute, or until golden. Add shrimp and tomatoes with their juice. Sauté for 4 minutes, or until heated through. Pour over pierogies.

**Makes 4 servings**

*Per serving: 403 calories, 27g protein, 44g carbohydrates, 13g fat, 3g saturated fat, 139mg cholesterol, 864mg sodium*

SuperQuick

# Mushroom Stroganoff

*Prep* **15 MINUTES** *Cook* **15 MINUTES**

- 5 ounces spinach fettuccine
- 1 tablespoon butter
- 1 pound mushrooms, sliced
- 1 medium onion, chopped
- 1 small garlic clove finely chopped
- 2 tablespoons all-purpose flour
- ¼ teaspoon ground black pepper
- 1 cup vegetable broth
- 2 tablespoons tomato paste
- ½ cup sour cream

*Named after Stroganov, a Russian diplomat, this richly flavored dish is usually made with beef tenderloin. Using mushrooms instead makes it much lighter (and just as delicious).*

**LET'S BEGIN** Cook the pasta according to package directions. Drain and keep warm.

**SAUTÉ IT** Meanwhile, melt the butter in a medium saucepan over medium heat until sizzling. Add the mushrooms, onion, and garlic and cook for 5 to 7 minutes, until the mushrooms are tender.

**MAKE IT SAUCY** Stir the flour and pepper into the mushroom mixture, then stir in the broth and tomato paste until blended. Cook, stirring constantly, for 2 to 3 minutes, until the mixture comes to a boil. Boil, stirring constantly, for 1 minute. Reduce the heat to low and stir in the sour cream. Cook for 1 to 2 minutes, until the mixture is heated through (do not let it boil!). Transfer the pasta to a large platter and top with the mushroom sour cream mixture.

**Makes 2 servings**

*Per serving: 490 calories, 18g protein, 66g carbohydrates, 20g fat, 11g saturated fat, 89mg cholesterol, 740mg sodium*

## Cooking Basics

### HOW TO SAUTÉ MUSHROOMS RIGHT

When sautéing mushrooms, heat the oil or butter in a heavy skillet over high heat. Avoid using a nonstick skillet, as the heat will not be as direct and mushrooms will not brown as well. Add the mushrooms, stirring constantly. Note they'll first give off a lot of water. Let it boil away, so the mushrooms don't stew in the liquid and turn gray. Instead, in a dry skillet, they'll cook to a rich brown.

SuperQuick

# Pasta Peanut Stir-fry

*Prep* **12 MINUTES** *Cook* **15 MINUTES**

- 1 pound linguine or thin spaghetti
- 1 teaspoon vegetable oil
- 4 carrots, cut into matchstick strips
- 1 large cucumber, peeled and cut into matchstick strips
- 1 bunch scallions, sliced diagonally into ½-inch lengths
- ½ teaspoon red pepper flakes

Peanut Sauce (see recipe)

*To save time in the kitchen, buy a bag of matchstick carrots, which are found in the produce section of supermarkets. Or use one of the new (and inexpensive) vegetable slicers.*

**LET'S BEGIN** Prepare the pasta according to package directions. Drain and keep warm.

**STIR-FRY** Meanwhile, heat the oil in a large nonstick wok or skillet over high heat. Stir-fry the carrots for 2 to 3 minutes, or until tender. Add the cucumbers, scallions, and pepper flakes and stir-fry for 2 minutes.

**MAKE IT SAUCY** Add the combined sauce ingredients to the wok and season to taste with pepper. Bring to a boil. Transfer the pasta to a large serving bowl and top with the vegetable mixture. Toss until mixed well.

## Peanut Sauce

*Combine ¼ cup reduced-sodium chicken broth, ¼ cup low-sodium soy sauce, ⅓ cup lime juice, and 3 tablespoons smooth peanut butter in a wok or saucepan. Season with black pepper. (Add in last step in recipe above.) Or, to use as a separate dipping sauce, bring to a boil over medium heat, stirring frequently, until the mixture comes to a full boil and thickens slightly.*

**Makes 4 servings**

*Per serving: 303 calories, 29g protein, 22g carbohydrates, 11g fat, 2g saturated fat, 90mg cholesterol, 1,239mg sodium*

SuperQuick

# Pork & Noodle Stir-Fry

Prep **10 MINUTES** Cook **15 MINUTES**

*Just eight simple ingredients put a tempting dinner on the table in minutes. Toasting sesame seeds brings out all of their nuttiness, but if you're short on time, leave them out.*

- 1 teaspoon vegetable oil
- 1 pound pork tenderloin, cut into stir-fry strips
- 1 package (16 ounces) frozen Oriental vegetable blend
- 2 packages (3½ ounces each) ramen noodles, broken into pieces
- 1½ cups water
- 3 tablespoons soy sauce
- 1½ teaspoons dark sesame oil
- 1 tablespoon toasted sesame seeds (optional)

**LET'S BEGIN** Heat the oil in a large nonstick skillet over medium-high heat.

**STIR-FRY** Stir-fry the pork for 5 minutes, or until it is lightly browned. Add all the remaining ingredients except the sesame seeds and bring to a boil.

**SIMMER & SERVE** Reduce the heat and simmer, stirring occasionally, for 4 to 5 minutes, until the noodles are completely soft and the vegetables are crisp-tender. Sprinkle with sesame seeds, if you like, and serve.

***Makes 4 servings***

*Per serving: 303 calories, 29g protein, 22g carbohydrates, 11g fat, 2g saturated fat, 90mg cholesterol, 1,239mg sodium*

## Cooking Basics

### HOW CAN I RESCUE MY PASTA POT?

**SERVE PASTA FAST!**
If pasta has to wait for the sauce to finish cooking, it's likely to become sticky and gluey, so make the sauce first. If cooked pasta must stand a few minutes, toss it with a little warm olive oil to coat it, while it waits.

**HOW TO UNSTICK PASTA**
If pasta clumps together into a gluey mass, all's not lost. Don't throw it out. Instead, submerge the pasta completely in hot water and separate. It'll be ready to serve in minutes.

**IS PASTA OVERCOOKED?**
Let's face it, an occasional pot of pasta can become overcooked and too soft. When this happens, forget about tossing the pasta with the sauce. It's likely to fall apart. Instead, just spoon the sauce on top. Tip: Save the extras to use in the soup pot.

**HOW TO STRAIN RAVIOLI**
After cooking, ravioli is tender and easily torn. Use a flat mesh strainer or slotted spoon to lift each ravioli out of the boiling water, one by one. If some tear, just cover them with sauce or bread-crumbs. They'll still be delicious!

SuperQuick

# Couscous Salad with Dried Cherries

*Prep* **10 MINUTES** *Cook* **5 MINUTES + 15 MINUTES STANDING**

- 1 cup water or chicken broth
- 3/4 cup couscous
- 1/2 cup dried tart cherries
- 1/2 cup coarsely chopped carrots
- 1/2 cup chopped unpeeled cucumber
- 1/4 cup sliced scallions
- 1/4 cup pine nuts or slivered almonds, toasted (optional)
- 3 tablespoons balsamic vinegar
- 1 tablespoon olive oil
- 1 tablespoon Dijon mustard

Salt and ground black pepper (optional)

*Dried fruit and couscous is a classic combination. Dried tart cherries make this dish special. If you have the time, be sure to toast the nuts, which brings out all their flavor—it adds crunch too.*

**LET'S BEGIN** Bring the water to a boil in a medium saucepan. Stir in the couscous and remove from the heat. Cover and let stand for 5 minutes, then fluff with a fork to separate the grains. Cool for 10 minutes.

**MIX IT UP** Toss the couscous and the next 5 ingredients together in a large bowl.

**SERVE** Combine the vinegar, oil, and mustard in a covered jar and shake until well blended. Pour over the couscous mixture, then stir until evenly coated. Season to taste with salt and pepper, if you like. Serve at room temperature or cover and refrigerate to serve later.

***Makes 6 servings***

*Per serving: 185 calories, 5g protein, 29g carbohydrates, 5g fat, 1g saturated fat, 0mg cholesterol, 65mg sodium*

SuperQuick

# Sesame-Ginger Noodles

*Prep* **12 MINUTES** *Cook* **10 MINUTES**

- 1 pound fresh Chinese-style thin egg noodles or vermicelli
- ½ cup water
- ¼ cup naturally brewed soy sauce
- 2 tablespoons distilled white vinegar
- 1 tablespoon sugar
- 1 teaspoon cornstarch
- 2 teaspoons grated, peeled fresh ginger
- 2 tablespoons vegetable oil
- ¾ cup sliced scallions
- 1 tablespoon sesame seeds, toasted
- ¾ teaspoon dark sesame oil

*Naturally brewed soy sauce is made with only three ingredients–soybeans, wheat, and salt–and no chemicals. It keeps longest in the refrigerator, where it will retain its flavor for a year.*

**LET'S BEGIN** Cook the noodles according to package directions, omitting the salt. Drain, rinse under cold running water, and drain thoroughly. Combine the next six ingredients in a small bowl and set aside.

**STIR-FRY** Heat the oil in a wok or large skillet over high heat. Stir-fry the scallions for 10 seconds. Add the soy-sauce mixture and stir-fry until the sauce thickens and boils. Add the noodles and stir-fry for 1 minute, or until the sauce returns to a boil and the noodles are evenly coated.

**TOSS IT UP** Add the sesame seeds and oil and toss well to combine. Serve straight from the wok or skillet.

***Makes 6 servings***

*Per serving: 362 calories, 12g protein, 59g carbohydrates, 9g fat, 1g saturated fat, 0mg cholesterol, 705mg sodium*

## Food Facts

### 5 Different Asian Noodles

In many Asian countries, noodles are not generally made from wheat, as in the United States, but from rice flour or vegetable starches, like soybean or potato. Here are a few:

**Cellophane noodles, also bean threads:** These see-through noodles are made from mung beans. They need soaking before using in most dishes. Drop right out of the package into soups.

**Ramen or Chinese-style egg noodles:** These deep-fried noodles are made from wheat flour and sold in cellophane packages, with a powder for making a tasty broth.

**Rice sticks, also rice flour noodles or vermicelli:** These long thin translucent noodles need soaking before being cooked or deep-fried.

**Soba:** These Japanese noodles are made from buckwheat and wheat flour, giving them a brownish-grey color. Square, medium-thick buckwheat noodles are great in soups.

**Wonton Wrappers:** These Chinese noodles are bite-size dumplings (small pillows of doug) resemble ravioli. Wontons are filled with meat, seafood, or vegetables and are boiled, steamed, or deep fried. Use to replace noodles in lasagna.

SuperQuick

# SNAKE ALLEY NOODLES

*Prep* **12 MINUTES** *Cook* **15 MINUTES**

- 12 ounces spaghetti
- 1 cup water
- ¼ cup naturally brewed soy sauce
- 2 tablespoons dry sherry
- 4 teaspoons cornstarch
- 1 pound ground pork
- 1 tablespoon minced, peeled fresh ginger
- 2 garlic cloves, minced
- ½ teaspoon red pepper flakes
- ¾ cup chopped scallions
- 8 ounces cooked baby shrimp, rinsed and drained

*There are several quick and easy ways to peel fresh ginger. You can use a vegetable peeler, or you can scrape the peel away using the tip of a serving teaspoon. It works surprisingly well.*

**LET'S BEGIN** Cook the spaghetti according to package directions, omitting the salt. Drain and keep warm.

**STIR-FRY** Meanwhile, combine the water, soy sauce, sherry, and cornstarch in a measuring cup. Heat a wok or large skillet over medium-high heat. Stir-fry the pork, ginger, garlic, and pepper flakes for 5 minutes, or until the pork is cooked through. Add the scallions and stir-fry for 1 minute.

**BUBBLE & STIR** Add the soy sauce mixture to the wok. Stir-fry for 2 minutes, or until the sauce thickens and bubbles. Add the shrimp and stir-fry for 1 minute, or until heated through. Transfer the pasta and shrimp mixture to a large serving bowl and toss until mixed well.

***Makes 4 to 6 servings***

*Per serving: 715 calories, 43g protein, 71g carbohydrates, 26g fat, 9g saturated fat, 167mg cholesterol, 1,188mg sodium*

SuperQuick

# Indonesian Pork Noodle Bowl

*Prep* **15 MINUTES** *Cook* **13 MINUTES**

- **8 ounces vermicelli or angel hair pasta**
- **1 tablespoon vegetable oil**
- **1 pound boneless, single loin pork roast, cut into ¼-inch-thick strips**
- **2 garlic cloves, crushed**
- **½ teaspoon red pepper flakes**
- **2 cups coarsely shredded cabbage**
- **1 cup chopped celery**
- **2 green onions, sliced**
- **¼ cup soy sauce**

*Pork and noodles are both important ingredients in Indonesian cuisine. This bowl has the familiar thin noodles, along with the salty flavor of soy sauce and the heat of red pepper flakes.*

**LET'S BEGIN** Break the pasta into thirds and cook according to package directions. Drain and keep warm.

**INTO THE PAN** Heat 2 teaspoons of the oil in a large nonstick skillet over medium-high heat. Add the pork, garlic, and pepper flakes and stir-fry for 2 to 3 minutes, until the pork is no longer pink. Transfer the pork to a plate and keep warm.

**STIR-FRY & SERVE** Add the remaining teaspoon of oil to the skillet and stir-fry the cabbage, celery, and green onions for 1 to 2 minutes, until crisp-tender. Return the pork to the skillet along with the pasta. Stir until heated through.

***Makes 4 servings***

*Per serving: 442 calories, 34g protein, 48g carbohydrates, 12g fat, 3g saturated fat, 62mg cholesterol, 1,118mg sodium*

SuperQuick

# Chicken Zorba

*Prep* **10 MINUTES** *Cook* **15 MINUTES**

- 8 ounces orzo pasta
- 1 pound thinly sliced boneless, skinless, chicken breast cutlets
- 1 teaspoon dried oregano
- Salt and pepper
- 1 tablespoon olive oil
- 3 garlic cloves, crushed
- 1 can (14½ ounces) Italian-style tomatoes
- ½ teaspoon fennel seeds
- ½ cup crumbled feta cheese
- Chopped fresh parsley
- ⅓ cup Kalamata or other olives (optional)

*Fast-cook this chicken 'n' tomato dish, typical of the Greek Isles.*

**LET'S BEGIN** Cook orzo according to package directions. Drain. Season chicken with oregano, salt, and pepper. Heat oil in a large skillet over medium-high heat. Sauté the garlic for 2 minutes. Add chicken and brown, turning once, for 5 minutes.

**INTO THE PAN** Stir in the tomatoes and fennel. Reduce the heat to medium-low and simmer, uncovered, for 5 minutes. Serve the chicken and sauce over the orzo. Sprinkle with the feta and parsley, then garnish with olives, if you wish.

***Makes 4 servings***

*Per serving: 408 calories, 37g protein, 48g carbohydrates, 6g fat, 3g saturated fat, 82mg cholesterol, 546mg sodium*

SuperQuick

# Asian Chicken 'n' Noodles

*Prep* **10 MINUTES** *Cook* **5 MINUTES**

- **1 package (3 ounces) ramen noodles**
- **1 large carrot, thinly sliced**
- **1½ cups boiling water**
- **1 package (6 ounces) grilled chicken breast strips**
- **1 green onion, sliced**

*Serve supper in authentic Asian style, with this quick-cooking skillet dish that goes from shopping bag to table in just 15 minutes. It's all thanks to fast-cooking noodles and already-grilled chicken.*

**LET'S BEGIN** Add the noodles and carrot to a pot of boiling water over high heat. Cook for 3 minutes. Drain.

**INTO THE PAN** Return the noodles and carrot to the pan. Stir in 1 teaspoon of the seasoning packet and the chicken strips and heat through. Sprinkle with the onion.

***Makes 2 servings***

*Per serving: 237 calories, 29g protein, 16g carbohydrates, 6g fat, 1g saturated fat, 86mg cholesterol, 388mg sodium*

*Bistro Chicken Pasta Salad*, page 116

# Pasta Tosses

Pasta is just meant for tossing with all kinds of things. From a simple flavorful olive oil to a fast vinaigrette dressing or some shredded cheese or a tomato sauce straight from a jar, it's the sauce that transforms mild-flavored strands of linguine or even stuffed ravioli pockets into a delicious supper. Our collection has many such terrific fast tosses: a red wine vinaigrette for orzo salad, a mustard-cream for macaroni salad, and a rich Alfredo for ravioli. You'll also find a white clam sauce for spaghetti, a peanut sauce for linguine, and a Caesar dressing for ziti. Pick a recipe. Then mix up, simmer up, and toss up a sauce for some pasta, and you'll have dinner in a hurry with little fuss.

SuperQuick

# Apple Tortellini Salad

*Prep* **15 MINUTES** *Cook* **10 MINUTES**

- 1 package (9 ounces) cheese-filled tortellini (refrigerated or frozen)
- 3 medium sweet-tart apples
- 3 tablespoons frozen apple juice concentrate, thawed
- 3 tablespoons light corn syrup
- 2 teaspoons brown sugar
- 1 teaspoon apple cider vinegar
- ¼ teaspoon garlic salt
- Ground white pepper
- 2 cups shredded salad greens
- 1 cup sliced fresh strawberries
- ½ cup thinly sliced celery
- ½ cup sliced scallions
- 2 tablespoons toasted pine nuts

*Springtime is the perfect time for this fast, elegant, and easy salad, It uses Consider Romaine or iceberg lettuces, as these shred the best. For the quickest shredding, use a serrated bread knife.*

**LET'S BEGIN** Cook the tortellini according to package directions. Drain and cool by rinsing the pasta under cold water. Shake gently to drain thoroughly and place in a large bowl. Peel, core, and slice the apples and add to the bowl.

**MIX IT UP** Meanwhile, combine the apple juice concentrate, corn syrup, brown sugar, vinegar, garlic salt, and pepper in a screw-top jar; shake well and refrigerate.

**TOSS & SERVE** Combine the tortellini, apples, salad greens, strawberries, celery, and scallions in a large bowl. Toss the salad gently with dressing. Sprinkle with the pine nuts.

***Makes 6 to 8 servings***

*Per serving: 253 calories, 8g protein, 47g carbohydrates, 5g fat, 2g saturated fat, 23mg cholesterol, 349mg sodium*

## Time Savers

### 3 WAYS TO SPEED UP PASTA TOSSES

**1. Buy fresh pasta** instead of dried if you're in a hurry and time is precious. Expect to pay extra for the convenience

**2. Prepare double or triple amounts of the sauce** beforehand. Then store the extras in the refrigerator or freezer. At suppertime, use your microwave to warm the sauce (and defrost if necessary), while you're boiling the water for the pasta.

**3. When using dried pasta,** pre-cook it until it's almost but not quite done. Interrupt the cooking process by rinsing under cold water, then toss with a little oil to avoid clumping. To serve, toss back into boiling water a minute or two until pasta is piping hot.

## On the Menu

**Here's a buffet supper that waits for your guests. Serve dishes at room temperature.**

*Assorted Grilled Veggies*

*Roasted Pork Loin with Brown-Sugar Glaze*

*Orzo Salad*

*Marinated Tomatoes & Cucumbers*

*Ciabatta Rolls with Herb Butter*

*Cranberry Juice Sparklers*

*Red Grapes with Brie*

SuperQuick

# Orzo Salad

*Prep* **12 MINUTES** *Cook* **15 MINUTES**

*Orzo is the Italian for "barley," which makes excellent salads. To speed up assembly time near dinnertime, make the orzo ahead, drain it, and refrigerate.*

- **1 cup orzo**
- **3 tablespoons olive oil**
- **3 tablespoons red wine vinegar**
- **½ teaspoon sugar**
- **¼ teaspoon salt**
- **¾ cup cherry-flavored dried cranberries**
- **2 scallions, sliced**
- **⅓ cup slivered almonds, toasted**

**LET'S BEGIN** Cook the orzo according to package directions. Drain the orzo and rinse under cold water until cool, then drain again. Put in a serving bowl.

**MIX IT UP** Meanwhile, whisk the oil, vinegar, sugar, and salt together in a small bowl until blended.

**TOSS & SERVE** Add the dried cranberries, scallions, and almonds to the orzo in the serving bowl. Drizzle over the dressing and toss until evenly coated. Serve at room temperature or cover and refrigerate for up to several hours.

***Makes 4 servings***

*Per serving: 400 calories, 8g protein, 54g carbohydrates, 16g fat, 2g saturated fat, 0mg cholesterol, 147mg sodium*

# GRILLED CHICKEN PASTA TOSS

*Prep* **15 MINUTES + MARINATING** *Cook* **23 MINUTES**

- 8 ounces fettuccine or linguine
- 6 boneless, skinless chicken breast halves
- 1 bottle (12 ounces) herb and garlic marinade with lemon juice
- 2 tablespoons vegetable oil
- 1½ cups broccoli florets
- 1 cup snow peas, trimmed
- 1 cup diagonally sliced carrots
- 1 can (2¼ ounces) sliced ripe black olives, drained

*Here's a grilled chicken and pasta toss that is dinner-in-a-bowl. "Pretty up" the carrots by using a zigzag-bladed knife to slice them.*

**LET'S BEGIN** Cook the pasta according to package directions. Drain. Marinate chicken in 1 cup marinade for at least 30 minutes in the refrigerator. Reserve rest of marinade.

**FIRE UP THE GRILL** Grill the chicken over hot coals, brushing with 2 tablespoons of the marinade, for 5 minutes, or until the juices run clear. Slice the chicken and keep warm.

**INTO THE PAN** Heat the oil in a medium skillet over medium-high heat. Sauté the broccoli, snow peas, and carrots. Cook for 3 minutes, or until crisp-tender. Combine the vegetables, olives, pasta, and chicken in a large serving bowl. Pour the remaining marinade over and toss gently to evenly coat.

***Makes 4 to 6 servings***

*Per serving: 406 calories, 44g protein, 30g carbohydrates, 11g fat, 2g saturated fat, 99mg cholesterol, 1,404mg sodium*

SuperQuick

# Ravioli Alfredo

*Prep* **12 MINUTES** *Cook* **10 MINUTES**

- 1 package (9 ounces) four-cheese ravioli, cooked and drained
- 1 package (10 ounces) Alfredo sauce
- 1 jar (7 ounces) roasted red bell peppers, drained and sliced
- ⅓ cup walnut pieces, toasted plus extra for garnish

Chopped fresh parsley (optional)

*Walnuts are really easy to toast, and they are a quick way to add crunch and flavor. Put them in a dry skillet and cook over medium heat until toasted, shaking the pan and tossing them often.*

**LET'S BEGIN** Cook the pasta according to package directions. Drain and keep warm.

**SIMMER & TOSS** Meanwhile, stir the ⅓ cup Alfredo sauce, peppers, and walnuts in a large saucepan over medium heat for 5 minutes or until hot. Pour over the ravioli and toss to coat. Garnish with extra walnuts and parsley, if you like.

***Makes 4 servings***

*Per serving: 443 calories, 14g protein, 31g carbohydrates, 30g fat, 9g saturated fat, 51mg cholesterol, 659mg sodium*

## Food Facts

### Circa 1914: The Creation of Fettuccine Alfredo

Not surprising, Fettuccine Alfredo was created by Alfredo Di Lelio, owner of his own restaurant in Rome, Italy, in the early 1900s. In 1914, he created a dish with a very rich triple butter (no cream), three kinds of flour, and the best Parmigiano. It came to be known as Fettuccine all'Alfredo. In 1927, movie actors Douglas Fairbanks and Mary Pickford dined at Alfredo's daily, while they honeymooned in Rome. The stars presented Alfredo a gold-plated spoon and fork (to mix his noodles with), with the inscription "To Alfredo, the King of the Noodles, July 1927." The international press spread Alfredo's noodle fame around the world. Within a year, a recipe appeared in the U.S. in a cookbook by George Rector.

After World War II, Alfredo moved his restaurant to the Piazza Augusto Imperatore. Thanks to the now-famous noodle dish, Alfredo's soon acquired that "must visit" status among Americans visiting Rome. Their love of the dish is still alive.

Over the years, Americans have not been able to find the rich butter, like the one used by Alfredo in his original creation. So, cooks began adding rich heavy cream. Today, most all Fettuccine Alfredos contain heavy cream.

SuperQuick

# Ravioli with Creamy Spinach Sauce

*Prep* **12 MINUTES** *Cook* **15 MINUTES**

- 1 package (24 ounces) frozen ravioli
- 1 box (10 ounces) frozen chopped spinach
- 1 jar ($14\frac{1}{2}$ ounces) Alfredo pasta sauce
- $\frac{1}{4}$ teaspoon ground nutmeg
- 1 cup chopped tomato or roasted red pepper

*Refrigerated ravioli works just as well as frozen in this creamy recipe. Follow the directions on the box for easy cooking. Just about any favorite ravioli filling will work here.*

**LET'S BEGIN** Cook the ravioli according to package directions. Drain and keep warm. Cook the spinach according to package directions. Place in a strainer and press out the excess moisture with the back of a spoon.

**INTO THE PAN** Combine the spinach, Alfredo sauce, and nutmeg in the pasta pot. Cook over medium heat for 4 minutes, or until heated through.

**TOSS & SERVE** Add the ravioli and tomato to the spinach mixture and gently toss to mix.

***Makes 4 servings***

*Per serving: 914 calories, 34g protein, 72g carbohydrates, 56g fat, 30g saturated fat, 129mg cholesterol, 1,176mg sodium*

## Food Facts

### Great Beginnings: The Story of Caesar Salad

According to history, Caesar salad originated in a restaurant in Tijuana, Mexico called Caesar's Place. As the story goes, one evening, Caesar Cardini, the restaurant's owner and chef, was pretty much out of food. He made up a salad from the ingredients he found in the kitchen: romaine lettuce, a hunk of Romano cheese, some bread, olive oil, and egg. He tore the lettuce into bite-size pieces, fried up some croutons, grated some of the cheese, rubbed the salad bowl with garlic, and whipped up a lemony dressing that included a coddled egg—but no anchovies! The salad as a huge hit and the rest is history—good-eating history.

SuperQuick

# Caesar Shrimp & Pasta

*Prep* **15 MINUTES** *Cook* **13 MINUTES**

- 8 ounces ziti, mostaccioli (moustaches), or other medium pasta
- 3 cups broccoli florets
- ⅓ cup + 2 tablespoons light Caesar salad dressing
- 12 ounces uncooked peeled and deveined shrimp, thawed if frozen
- ¼ teaspoon crushed red hot pepper flakes
- ¼ cup grated Romano cheese

*Here Caesar salad is made even better with broccoli, shrimp, and cheese. To save time, buy precut florets, cooked and cleaned shrimp, and grated Romano cheese.*

**LET'S BEGIN** Prepare the pasta according to package directions. Add broccoli florets 3 minutes before the pasta is done. Drain, transfer to a bowl, and keep warm.

**STIR-FRY** Meanwhile, heat the 2 tablespoons dressing in a large skillet over medium-high heat. Stir-fry shrimp and pepper flakes for 3 minutes or until shrimp is opaque.

**TOSS IT UP** Add the shrimp to the pasta and broccoli. Drizzle over the remaining ⅓ cup of dressing and toss well. Sprinkle with the cheese.

***Makes 4 servings***

*Per serving: 372 calories, 24g protein, 47g carbohydrates, 9g fat, 2g saturated fat, 131mg cholesterol, 825mg sodium*

## Cook to Cook

### WHICH PASTAS DO YOU TOSS INTO SALADS?

"When I'm making a pasta salad, I always use pastas that are ***strong enough to hold their shape when being tossed*** in the salad bowl. Also, most pasta salads marinate for several hours in a salad dressing, so they need to be able to stand up and stay firm during this time, too.

I look for ***pastas with fun and unusual shapes when making salads.*** *Farfalle* in the shape of butterflies are perfect because their "wings" hold extra droplets of salad dressing or even tiny salad ingredients such as peas. They're also called bow ties, for they look like just like them.

Try the pasta that ***looks like little radiators, called radiatore.*** Their edges are rippled and grab onto the salad dressing easily, plus they're hearty enough to be tossed again and again.

I've found that other pastas are great for salads too, such as ***ruote, which are shaped like little wheels with spokes.*** And *rotini*, which are spirals of pasta that look like corkscrews. These hold the droplets of dressing well, too."

# MINESTRONE PASTA SALAD

*Prep* **15 MINUTES + CHILLING** *Cook* **12 MINUTES**

*In Italian,* minestrone *means "big soup" and refers to a soup that usually contains pasta and beans or peas. This salad, by the same name, uses* ruote *or wagon-wheel pasta and red kidney beans. Make the salad quicker by using drained diced canned tomatoes.*

- **1 cup ruote or rotelle (wagon wheels and cartwheels) or rotini (corkscrews)**
- **1 can (19 ounces) red kidney beans, rinsed and drained**
- **3 medium tomatoes, seeded and chopped**
- **2 green bell peppers, chopped**
- **2 scallions, chopped**
- **½ cup Italian dressing**
- **½ cup shredded Cheddar cheese**

**LET'S BEGIN** Cook the pasta according to package directions. Drain, rinse under cold running water, and drain again. Mix the pasta, beans, tomatoes, bell peppers, and scallions together in a serving bowl.

**TOSS & CHILL** Add the Italian dressing, tossing to coat. Cover and refrigerate for several hours or overnight

**SERVE** Just before serving, toss the salad and sprinkle with the cheese.

***Makes 6 servings***

*Per serving: 277 calories, 10g protein, 31g carbohydrates, 13g fat, 3g saturated fat, 10mg cholesterol, 527mg sodium*

# Pork Linguine Salad

*Prep* **15 MINUTES + MARINATING** *Cook* **15 MINUTES**

- 1 pound boneless pork chops
- ½ cup citrus grill marinade with orange juice
- 8 ounces linguine, broken in half
- 1 tablespoon vegetable oil
- ½ small red onion, thinly sliced
- ½ large red bell pepper, thinly sliced
- 4 ounces snow peas, trimmed
- 2 tablespoons finely chopped fresh parsley
- ½ teaspoon lemon pepper
- ½ teaspoon seasoned salt

Citrus Dressing (see recipe)

*Boneless pork chops are usually available thin cut and regular cut, which are about ¾ inch thick and are best here. For easier cutting, pop them into the freezer for 30 minutes.*

**LET'S BEGIN** Cut the pork into thin strips, ¼-inch wide. Combine the pork and citrus grill marinade in a resealable plastic bag. Press out the air and marinate in the refrigerator for 30 minutes. Cook the pasta according to package directions. Drain and keep warm.

**STIR-FRY** Remove the meat from the bag and discard the marinade. Heat the oil in a large skillet over medium-high heat. Sauté the pork for 5 minutes, or until cooked through. Transfer the pork to a bowl. Add the onion, bell pepper, snow peas, parsley, lemon pepper, and seasoned salt to the skillet. Cook for 4 minutes, or until the onion is tender.

**MAKE IT SAUCY** Return the pork to the skillet with the pasta and sauté for 3 minutes, or until heated through. Transfer to a large serving bowl. Drizzle with dressing and toss to coat.

## Citrus Dressing

*Whisk together ¼ cup citrus grill marinade with orange juice, ¼ cup fresh lemon juice, ¼ cup vegetable oil, and ½ teaspoon lemon pepper.*

***Makes 4 servings***

*Per serving: 590 calories, 33g protein, 54g carbohydrates, 25g fat, 5g saturated fat, 62mg cholesterol, 748mg sodium*

SuperQuick

# TANGY PASTA SALAD

*Prep* **15 MINUTES + CHILLING** *Cook* **15 MINUTES**

- 16 ounces mostaccioli (little moustaches) or rotini (corkscrews)
- 6 slices bacon
- 1¼ cups salad dressing
- 2 tablespoons sugar
- ½ teaspoon garlic salt
- 3 carrots, shredded
- 1 red or yellow onion, sliced
- 1 green bell pepper, chopped

*German immigrants were especially good at taking advantage of flavorful bacon drippings when making potato salad and green salad. And, it works its magic here as well.*

**LET'S BEGIN** Cook the pasta according to package directions. Drain. Cook the bacon in a medium skillet until crisp. Transfer the bacon to paper towels to drain, then crumble. Reserve the bacon drippings.

**TOSS & CHILL** Combine 2 tablespoons of the reserved bacon drippings, the salad dressing, sugar, and garlic salt in a large serving bowl. Add the pasta and all the remaining ingredients except the bacon, mixing gently. Cover and refrigerate for several hours or overnight.

**SERVE** Sprinkle with the bacon just before serving.

**Makes 8 servings**

*Per serving: 412 calories, 10g protein, 59g carbohydrates, 16g fat, 3g saturated fat, 14mg cholesterol, 409mg sodium*

SuperQuick

# Spaghetti with White Clam Sauce

Prep **12 MINUTES** Cook **10 MINUTES**

- 1 package (16 ounces) spaghetti or linguine
- 2 tablespoons vegetable oil
- 2 garlic cloves, minced
- 2 cans (6½ ounces each) chopped clams, drained, liquid reserved
- ½ cup chopped fresh parsley
- ¼ cup dry white wine or chicken broth
- 1 teaspoon dried basil
- ¼ ground white or black pepper

*There are lots of easy ways to vary this popular pasta dish. Add some freshly grated lemon zest to the skillet along with the parsley, toss in a pinch of crushed red pepper, or thinly slice some fresh basil leaves (instead of the dried).*

**LET'S BEGIN** Cook the pasta according to package directions. Drain, transfer to a serving bowl, and keep warm.

**INTO THE PAN** Heat the oil in a large skillet over medium-high heat. Sauté the garlic for 1 minute. Stir in the reserved clam liquid and parsley. Cook, stirring for 3 minutes, or until bubbly. Add the clams, wine, basil, and pepper.

**SIMMER & TOSS** Reduce the heat to low. Simmer sauce for 5 minutes, or until heated through. Pour over pasta.

**Makes 8 servings**

*Per serving: 317 calories, 19g protein, 45g carbohydrates, 5g fat, 1g saturated fat, 31mg cholesterol, 58mg sodium*

## Cook to Cook

### CAN I SUBSTITUTE FRESH CLAMS FOR CANNED ONES IN A RECIPE?

"Yes, it's easy to use fresh clams instead of canned ones in a recipe. **Buy the smallest ones, called littleneck clams.** Ask your fishmonger to shuck them for you if he has the time (it's worth the little extra you'll pay for the convenience). Also, ask him to add a little broth, too, if he has it. For each 6½-ounce can of clams called for in the recipe, use a dozen shucked littlenecks. If the liquid from the cans is used in the recipe and the fresh clams do not have any broth, substitute bottled clam juice or homemade or canned chicken broth."

SuperQuick

# Shrimp & Artichoke Linguine

Prep **15 MINUTES** Cook **15 MINUTES**

- 8 ounces linguine
- 2 tablespoons vegetable oil
- 1 medium onion, chopped
- 1 large garlic clove, minced
- 1 pound large shrimp, peeled and deveined
- 1 package (9 ounces) frozen artichoke hearts
- 1 cup white wine or chicken broth
- 2 teaspoons grated lemon zest
- 2 tablespoons lemon juice
- 1 teaspoon hot pepper sauce
- ½ teaspoon salt
- 2 tablespoons chopped fresh parsley

*Using frozen artichoke hearts instead of fresh ones in this recipe cuts preparation considerably. They're just as tasty as the fresh—and cost less, too.*

**LET'S BEGIN** Cook the pasta according to package directions. Drain and keep warm. Meanwhile, heat the oil in a large skillet over medium heat. Sauté the onion and garlic for 5 minutes, or until tender. Transfer to a small bowl with a slotted spoon.

**BUBBLE & STIR** Add the shrimp to the drippings remaining in the skillet. Cook over medium-high heat for 3 minutes or until the shrimp turn pink. Stir in the frozen artichoke hearts, white wine, lemon zest and juice, hot pepper sauce, salt, and onion mixture. Heat to boiling over high heat.

**SEASON & TOSS** Reduce the heat to low. Cover and simmer for 5 minutes to blend flavors. Toss the artichoke mixture with the linguine. Sprinkle with the parsley and serve.

**Makes 2 servings**

*Per serving: 940 calories, 65g protein, 108g carbohydrates, 20g fat, 3g saturated fat, 345mg cholesterol, 1,072mg sodium*

SuperQuick

# Broccoli-Walnut Noodles

*Prep* **12 MINUTES** *Bake* **12 MINUTES**

- 12 ounces extra wide curly "no yolk" noodles
- 2 pounds broccoli
- 2 tablespoons olive oil
- ½ cup chopped California walnuts
- Grated zest and juice of 1 lemon
- Juice of ½ orange
- ½ teaspoon ground black pepper

*Curly noodles are fun—they even keep their curly shape when cooked. If you don't have an orange on hand, substitute about 3 tablespoons good-quality orange juice.*

**LET'S BEGIN** Cook the noodles according to package directions. Drain, transfer to a large bowl, and keep warm.

**COOK & CUT** Meanwhile, steam the broccoli in 1 inch of boiling water in a large pot for 3 to 5 minutes, or until tender. Drain and cool slightly. Cut broccoli into small florets, then peel the stems and cut into ½-inch-thick slices.

**SAUTÉ & SERVE** Heat olive oil over medium-high heat. Sauté the walnuts for 1 minute, or until fragrant. Add broccoli to noodles and drizzle with the walnut-oil mixture, and toss well. Add the remaining ingredients and toss again.

***Makes 4 servings***

*Per serving: 644 calories, 20g protein, 80g carbohydrate, 19g total fat, 2g saturated fat, 0mg cholesterol, 8mg sodium*

SuperQuick

# Bistro Chicken Pasta Salad

Prep **15 MINUTES** Cook **10 MINUTES**

- 1 cup penne
- 2 grilled or broiled boneless, skinless chicken breast halves
- ½ cup Italian dressing mix for nonfat dressing
- 1 cup quartered cherry tomatoes
- 1 package (4 ounces) traditional crumbled feta cheese
- ⅓ cup fresh basil leaves, thinly sliced
- ¼ cup chopped red onion
- ¼ cup chopped sun-dried tomatoes (not oil-packed)

*This salad is a great way to use up leftover cooked chicken breasts, or grill up a few extra pieces of chicken the next time you fire up the barbecue. Or, pick up some precooked ones at your grocer's.*

**LET'S BEGIN** Cook the pasta according to package directions. Drain and keep warm. Cut the chicken into ¼-inch-thick slices. Prepare the salad dressing mix according to package directions for nonfat dressing.

**TOSS & SERVE** Toss all the ingredients except the chicken together in a serving bowl. Top with the chicken. Serve warm or chilled.

***Makes 4 servings***

*Per serving: 244 calories, 21g protein, 22g carbohydrates, 8g fat, 5g saturated fat, 62mg cholesterol, 710mg sodium*

SuperQuick

# PASTA WITH TURKEY SAUSAGE & OLIVES

*Prep* **12 MINUTES** *Cook* **15 MINUTES**

- 1 pound mostaccioli or rigatoni
- 8 ounces Italian-style turkey sausage
- 1 tablespoon olive or vegetable oil
- 1 garlic clove, minced
- 2 cups canned plum tomatoes, crushed
- 12 medium black olives, pitted and sliced
- Pinch of red pepper flakes
- Salt and ground black pepper
- 2 tablespoons chopped fresh flat-leaf parsley
- Grated Parmesan cheese (optional)

*Save chopping time: use canned diced tomatoes. Italian-flavored turkey sausage is easy on the purse and the waistline.*

**LET'S BEGIN** Cook the pasta according to package directions. Drain, reserving 1 cup pasta water. Spray a medium skillet with nonstick cooking spray. Cook and stir the sausage over medium heat for 10 minutes, until cooked and drain.

**INTO THE PAN** Heat the oil in the same skillet over medium heat. Sauté the garlic for 1 minute, or until golden. Add the tomatoes, olives, and red pepper flakes. Return the sausage to the skillet and season with salt and pepper. Reduce the heat and simmer for 5 minutes, or until the sauce thickens. Toss with pasta, adding some reserved pasta water, if the sauce is too thick. Stir in the parsley. Top with cheese if you wish.

***Makes 4 to 6 servings***

*Per serving: 668 calories, 24g protein, 94g carbohydrates, 23g fat, 6g saturated fat, 30mg cholesterol, 695mg sodium*

SuperQuick

# Citrus-Cherry Pork & Pasta Salad

Prep **10 MINUTES** Cook **20 MINUTES**

- 8 ounces penne (or other small pasta)
- 3 cups broccoli florets

Orange Vinaigrette (see recipe)

- 1 teaspoon vegetable oil
- 1 whole pork tenderloin, about 1 pound, cut into ½-inch cubes
- ½ sweet yellow onion, thinly sliced
- ½ cup dried cherries
- ⅓ cup walnuts, coarsely chopped

*Using pork tenderloin in a pasta salad is terrific, especially when it's drizzled with a mild orange vinaigrette dressing. The flavors blend perfectly. Speed up the preparation by making the dressing ahead.*

**LET'S BEGIN** Prepare the pasta according to package directions, adding the broccoli during the last 3 minutes of cooking. Drain, rinse under cold water, and drain again. Prepare the dressing.

**INTO THE PAN** Heat the oil in a large nonstick skillet over high heat. Sauté the pork and onion for 4 to 5 minutes, until the pork is lightly browned and the onion is tender. Transfer to a large serving bowl.

**TOSS & SERVE** Add the pasta and broccoli, the cherries, and walnuts to the bowl with the pork and onion. Drizzle with the Orange Vinaigrette and toss to coat.

## Orange Vinaigrette

*To make this dressing, whisk together 2 tablespoons orange juice, 2 tablespoons balsamic vinegar, 2 tablespoons olive oil, 1 tablespoon grated orange zest, 2 tablespoons orange juice, ¼ teaspoon salt, and ¼ teaspoon ground black pepper.*

**Makes 6 servings**

*Per serving: 378 calories, 23g protein, 42g carbohydrates, 13g fat, 2g saturated fat, 49mg cholesterol, 150mg sodium*

SuperQuick

# Italian Chicken Pasta

*Prep* **12 MINUTES** *Cook* **12 MINUTES**

*Chicken breast halves cut into stir-fry strips for stir-frying available in many supermarkets and really speed up the time it will take to prepare this dish, while the beef seasoning flavors it up just right.*

- **8 ounces penne**
- **2 tablespoons olive oil**
- **1 pound boneless, skinless chicken breasts, cut into 1-inch-thick strips**
- **3 tablespoons beef seasoning**
- **Parmesan cheese (optional)**

**LET'S BEGIN** Cook the pasta according to package directions. Drain, rinse under cool water, and drain again.

**INTO THE PAN** Meanwhile, heat the oil in a nonstick skillet over medium-high heat. Sauté the chicken and beef seasoning for 5 to 7 minutes, until chicken juices run clear.

**HEAT & TOSS** Reduce the heat to low. Stir in the cooked penne and heat through. Sprinkle with Parmesan cheese, if you like.

***Makes 6 servings***

*Per serving: 254 calories, 19g protein, 31g carbohydrates, 6g fat, 1g saturated fat, 34mg cholesterol, 311mg sodium*

# REUNION PASTA SALAD

*Prep* **15 MINUTES** *Cook* **12 MINUTES** *Chill* **2 HOURS**

1 pound penne

1 bag (16 ounces) frozen baby carrots, green and yellow beans

2 cups frozen broccoli florets

White Wine Vinaigrette (see recipe)

2 pounds boneless, skinless chicken breast halves

Salt and ground black pepper

1 package (8 ounces) sliced fresh mushrooms

2 large tomatoes, diced

*When the crowd is gathering, here's the perfect salad to toss together. Make it the day before and refrigerate overnight. It'll taste even better!*

**LET'S BEGIN** Cook the pasta according to package directions, adding the frozen vegetable mix (carrots and beans) and broccoli after 8 minutes of cooking. Return to a boil. Cook 3 to 4 minutes longer until pasta and vegetables are tender. Drain, rinse under cool water, and drain again. Meanwhile, prepare the White Wine Vinaigrette.

**INTO THE PAN** Spray a large nonstick skillet with nonstick cooking spray. Heat the skillet over medium-high heat for 1 minute. Sauté the chicken for 7 to 9 minutes, until juices run clear. Cut into bite-size chunks and season with salt and pepper.

**SEASON & TOSS** Combine pasta-vegetable mixture, chicken, mushrooms, and tomatoes. Drizzle the dressing over the salad and toss to coat. Cover and refrigerate at least 2 hours before serving.

## WHITE WINE VINAIGRETTE

*To make the dressing, whisk together ½ cup olive oil, ⅓ cup white wine vinegar, 1 teaspoon salt, 2 tablespoons slivered fresh basil leaves (or 1 teaspoon dried), 1 teaspoon dried oregano leaves, and 2 cloves minced garlic, if you like.*

**Makes 14 servings**

*Per serving: 292 calories, 21g protein, 31g carbohydrates, 9g fat, 1g saturated fat,38mg cholesterol, 327mg sodium*

# Best-Ever Macaroni Salad

*Prep* **15 MINUTES** *Cook* **9 MINUTES** *Chill* **30 MINUTES**

- 8 ounces medium shell pasta
- ⅓ cup reduced-fat sour cream
- ⅓ cup reduced-fat mayonnaise
- ⅓ cup deli-style mustard
- 1 tablespoon cider vinegar
- 3 cups cut-up bite-size vegetables, such as tomatoes, peppers, carrots, and/or celery
- ¼ cup minced scallions
- Salt and ground black pepper

*Macaroni salad is as all-American as apple pie, picnics, church suppers. A mix of sour cream, mayonnaise, and just enough mustard makes this version especially yummy.*

**LET'S BEGIN** Cook the pasta according to package directions using shortest cooking time. Drain, rinse under cold running water, and drain again.

**STIR IT IN** Combine the sour cream, mayonnaise, mustard, and vinegar in a serving bowl. Add the pasta, vegetables, and scallions, tossing gently to coat. Season to taste with salt and pepper.

**CHILL & TOSS** Cover and refrigerate for 30 minutes. Toss before serving.

***Makes 6 servings***

*Per serving: 211 calories, 6g protein, 37g carbohydrates, 3g fat, 1g saturated fat, 8mg cholesterol, 411mg sodium*

*Reunion Pasta Salad*

SuperQuick

# Vegetable Linguine with Peanut Sauce

*Prep* **15 MINUTES** *Cook* **15 MINUTES**

- 5 ounces linguine
- Peanut Sauce (see recipe)
- 1 tablespoon butter
- 1 small red bell pepper, sliced (1 cup)
- 3 ounces fresh pea pods, tips and strings removed, cut in half diagonally (1 cup)
- 1 medium carrot, thinly sliced (½ cup)
- 3 tablespoons peanuts

*Here's a great supper dish—linguine tossed with a peanut sauce and fresh vegetables. Add a fresh green salad and tall iced teas.*

**LET'S BEGIN** Cook linguine according to package directions. Drain and transfer to a bowl. Make the Peanut Sauce, drizzle over the linguine and toss well. Keep warm.

**INTO THE PAN** Meanwhile, melt the butter in a large skillet over medium-high heat until sizzling. Add the red bell pepper, pea pods, and carrot. Stir-fry for 3 to 5 minutes, until the vegetables are crisp-tender.

**TOSS & SERVE** Add the vegetables to pasta mixture and toss until well coated. Sprinkle with the peanuts.

## Peanut Sauce

*Combine ¼ cup peanut butter, ¼ cup water, 2 tablespoons rice vinegar (or white wine vinegar), 2 tablespoons soy sauce, ¼ teaspoon ground ginger, and ¼ teaspoon crushed red pepper. Stir until well blended.*

**Makes 2 servings**

*Per serving: 644 calories, 23g protein, 73g carbohydrates, 31g fat, 8g saturated fat, 16mg cholesterol, 1,260mg sodium*

*Four-Cheese Broccoli Bake, page 134*

# Weekend Bakes

Get ready for those smiles as you bring a dish of lasagna to the table—all layered up, melted, and bubbling. Here are those dishes that used to take many hours to prepare and bake. But now they need only minutes to mix. Then just pop them into the oven to bake on their own. You'll find a spaghetti and beef bake in an iron skillet, dripping with Cheddar and tomatoes, and a no-boil ziti that takes only six ingredients and just minutes to toss together. There are jumbo shells to stuff, vegetable-cheese combos to mix up, and even a beef pie in a spaghetti shell to bake. Once in the oven, these dishes meld and melt together into a signature dish that's bursting over with homemade goodness and flavor.

# No-Boil Lasagna

*Prep* **20 MINUTES** *Bake* **1 HOUR, 10 MINUTES**

- 2 containers (15 ounces each) ricotta cheese
- 8 ounces shredded mozzarella cheese (2 cups)
- ½ cup grated Parmesan cheese
- 2 large eggs
- 2 jars (32 ounces each) pasta sauce with meat
- 12 no-boil lasagna noodles

*No-boil lasagna noodles, which are a bit thinner than usual, are great. When topped with sauce, they cook right in the oven.*

**LET'S BEGIN** Preheat the oven to 375°F. Combine the ricotta, 1 cup of the mozzarella, ¼ cup of the Parmesan, and the eggs in a large bowl.

**LAYER IT EASY** Spread 1 cup of pasta sauce on the bottom of a 13×9-inch baking dish. Layer with 4 noodles, 1 cup pasta sauce, and one-half of the ricotta mixture, repeating once. Top with remaining 4 noodles and 2 cups pasta sauce.

**INTO THE OVEN** Cover tightly with foil and bake for 1 hour. Sprinkle with the remaining mozzarella and Parmesan. Bake the lasagna uncovered 10 minutes longer, or until the cheese melts. Let stand for 10 minutes for easier cutting. Heat the remaining pasta sauce and serve alongside.

***Makes 12 Servings***

*Per serving: 393 calories, 20g protein, 30g carbohydrates, 20g fat, 10g saturated fat, 95mg cholesterol, 1,035mg sodium*

## Food Facts

### A PASTA POT FULL OF FUN FACTS

- Who probably enjoyed the first pasta? The Chinese, as early as 5,000 B.C.
- Thomas Jefferson is credited with introducing macaroni to the US after bringing back a recipe from one of his European journeys. At a White House dinner on February 6, 1802, a pie called macaroni appeared on the menu.
- One billion pounds of spaghetti, stacked end to end, equals enough to circle the earth's equator almost nine times (over 212,500 miles).
- Worldwide, there are more than 600 shapes of pasta.

## Easy Classic Lasagna

*Prep* **20 MINUTES** *Cook/Bake* **55 MINUTES**

*Be sure to let this lasagna rest for at least 10 minutes before attempting to cut it into servings. The resting time allows it to settle, which makes slicing a breeze.*

- 9 lasagna noodles
- 1 pound ground beef
- 1 medium onion, chopped
- 1 jar (28 ounces) pasta sauce
- 1 container (16 ounces) cottage cheese
- 12 ounces shredded mozzarella cheese (3 cups)
- ½ cup grated Parmesan cheese

**LET'S BEGIN** Preheat the oven to 350°F. Cook the noodles according to package directions. Drain and place on a kitchen towel in one layer.

**COOK IT QUICK** Meanwhile, cook the meat in a large skillet over medium-high heat for 5 minutes, or until brown, breaking it up with a spoon. Drain off the fat. Add the onion and cook, stirring, for 5 minutes, or until tender. Stir in the pasta sauce and cover the pan. Reduce the heat and simmer, stirring occasionally, for 15 minutes.

**LAYER & BAKE** Layer 3 noodles, one-third of the meat sauce, one-third of the cottage cheese, and one-third of the mozzarella in a 13×9-inch baking dish, then repeat the layers two times. Top with the Parmesan. Bake for 30 minutes. Let the lasagna stand for 10 minutes for easier cutting.

***Makes 6 to 8 servings***

*Per serving: 648 calories, 44g protein, 39g carbohydrates, 34g fat, 16g saturated fat, 112mg cholesterol, 1,560mg sodium*

### *On the Menu*

***Pull out the checkered tablecloth and stage a casual lasagna supper for friends.***

*Fresh Mozzarella Balls with Fresh Basil*

*Easy Classic Lasagna*

*Herb-stuffed Mushrooms*

*Orange and Arugula Salad*

*Hot Garlic Twists*

*Lemon Tart*

# Iron Skillet Spaghetti

*Prep* **12 MINUTES** *Cook/Bake* **45 MINUTES**

- 1 pound spaghetti or linguine
- 1½ pounds ground beef
- 2 tablespoons vegetable oil
- 1 large onion, finely chopped
- 1 large garlic clove, minced
- 1 can (28 ounces) crushed tomatoes
- ¼ cup finely chopped fresh parsley
- 2 teaspoons dried oregano
- 8 ounces shredded low-fat Cheddar cheese (2 cups)

*If you wish, prepare this dish several hours ahead and refrigerate. Near suppertime, just pop the skillet into the oven to finish the cooking. This few hours of rest makes the dish taste even better.*

**LET'S BEGIN** Preheat the oven to 350°F. Cook the pasta according to package directions. Drain and keep warm. Meanwhile, cook the beef in a large oven-safe skillet over medium heat for 5 minutes, or until brown, breaking it up with a spoon. With a slotted spoon, transfer the meat to a bowl. Drain off the fat from the skillet.

**SAUTÉ & SIMMER** Heat the oil in the skillet and sauté the onion and garlic for 5 minutes, or until tender. Return the beef to the skillet along with the tomatoes, parsley, and oregano and simmer for 10 minutes. Add the pasta and 1 cup of cheese to the tomato mixture, stirring until mixed well. Sprinkle with the remaining cheese.

**INTO THE OVEN** Bake for 30 minutes, or until the top is crispy and the meat mixture is heated through.

***Makes 4 to 6 servings***

*Per serving: 1,064 calories, 64g protein, 104g carbohydrates, 42g fat, 15g saturated fat, 129mg cholesterol, 959mg sodium*

# Beef Burgundy

*Prep* **15 MINUTES** *Cook/Bake* **1¾ HOURS**

- 2½ pounds boneless beef round steak, trimmed and cut into 1-inch slices
- 4 garlic cloves, minced
- ½ cup chopped onion
- 2 cups Burgundy or other dry red wine
- 1 can (10¾ ounces) condensed cream of mushroom soup, undiluted
- 1½ cups dried tart cherries
- 2 jars (4½ ounces) button mushrooms, drained
- 1 cup pearl onions (fresh, frozen or canned)
- 3 tablespoons all-purpose flour
- ½ cup water
- 12 ounces farfalle (bowties) or medium egg noodles

*Here's a faster-made version of the French* boeuf bourguignon.

**LET'S BEGIN** Preheat the oven to 350°F. Coat an ovenproof Dutch oven with non-stick cooking spray; place over medium heat until hot. Sauté the steak for 8 to 10 minutes, or until meat is browned. Drain well; set aside.

**INTO THE PAN** Recoat the pan with cooking spray; and place over medium heat. Sauté the garlic and onion for 1 minute. Add in the wine and mushroom soup and bring to a boil. Return the steak to the pan with the cherries, mushrooms and pearl onions. Whisk the flour and water together in a small bowl until smooth, then into the steak mixture.

**INTO THE OVEN** Bake, covered, for 1½ hours, or until steak is tender and mixture is thickened. Meanwhile, cook the pasta according to package directions. Drain and keep hot. Serve the meat over noodles.

***Makes 8 servings***

*Per serving: 478 calories, 31g protein, 29g carbohydrates, 20g fat, 7g saturated fat, 90mg cholesterol, 471mg sodium*

## Beef & Mozzarella Pie

*Prep* **20 MINUTES** *Cook/Bake* **35 MINUTES**

- 8 ounces spaghetti
- 1 pound ground beef, cooked and drained
- 2 cups pasta sauce
- ½ cup grated Parmesan cheese
- 1 large egg, lightly beaten
- 8 ounces shredded mozzarella cheese (2 cups)

*Spaghetti makes a great crust for a meat pie. It is light and crispy. Only about an ounce per serving is used.*

**LET'S BEGIN** Preheat the oven to 350°F. Cook the pasta according to package directions. Drain and keep warm.

**COOK AND TOSS** Meanwhile, cook the beef in a large skillet over medium heat for 5 minutes, or until brown. Drain off the fat. Stir in the pasta sauce. Toss the cooked spaghetti, Parmesan, and egg together in a large bowl. Press into the bottom and up the side of a 9-inch pie plate, forming a crust. Spoon in the meat filling and top with the mozzarella.

**INTO THE OVEN** Bake the pie for 30 minutes, or until the mozzarella melts and the mixture is heated through. Let stand for 5 minutes for easier serving.

***Makes 8 servings***

*Per serving: 420 calories, 24g protein, 34g carbohydrates, 21g fat, 10g saturated fat, 91mg cholesterol, 550mg sodium*

## No-Boil Ziti

*Prep* **10 MINUTES** *Cook/Bake* **60 MINUTES**

- 1 jar (32 ounces) pasta sauce with meat
- 1½ cups water
- 1 container (15 ounces) ricotta cheese
- 8 ounces shredded mozzarella cheese (2 cups)
- ¼ cup grated Parmesan cheese
- 8 ounces ziti

*Baked ziti, a classic southern Italian dish, is often reserved only for Sunday supper in many Italian households. No wonder—it's great!*

**LET'S BEGIN** Preheat the oven to 400°F. Combine the pasta sauce and water in a large bowl. Stir in the ricotta, 1 cup of the mozzarella, the Parmesan cheese, and the uncooked ziti. Spoon into a 13×9-inch baking dish. Cover tightly with foil.

**INTO THE OVEN** Bake for 55 minutes. Sprinkle with the remaining 1 cup mozzarella. Bake uncovered for 5 minutes longer. Let the ziti stand for 10 minutes for easier serving.

***Makes 8 servings***

*Per serving: 367calories, 19g protein, 31g carbohydrates, 18g fat, 10g saturated fat, 55mg cholesterol, 823mg sodium*

*Beef & Mozzarella Pie*

# FOUR-CHEESE BROCCOLI BAKE

*Prep* **12 MINUTES** *Cook/Bake* **35 MINUTES**

*This decadently rich dish has four great cheeses: ricotta, Parmesan, blue cheese, and mozzarella. Buying them already crumbled or shredded makes this dish easy to put together.*

- 1 pound farfalle (bow ties)
- 1 tablespoon olive oil
- 1 can (8 ounces) sliced mushrooms, drained
- 4 scallions, sliced
- 3 garlic cloves, minced
- 1 cup part-skim ricotta cheese
- ½ cup grated Parmesan cheese
- ½ cup blue cheese
- 1 cup milk
- 8 ounces shredded mozzarella cheese (2 cups)
- 1 package (10 ounces) frozen broccoli florets, thawed and drained

**LET'S BEGIN** Preheat the oven to 375°F. Cook the pasta according to package directions. Drain and keep warm.

**SAUTÉ IT QUICKLY** Meanwhile, heat the oil in a large skillet over medium heat. Sauté the mushrooms, scallions, and garlic for 5 minutes, or until tender. Stir in the ricotta, Parmesan, blue cheese, and milk until well blended. Toss the pasta, cheese mixture, mozzarella, and broccoli together in a large bowl.

**INTO THE OVEN** Spoon the pasta mixture into a 2-quart casserole. Bake for 20 to 25 minutes, until the mixture is heated through.

***Makes 6 servings***

*Per serving: 585 calories, 31g protein, 67g carbohydrates, 21g fat, 12g saturated fat, 61mg cholesterol, 650mg sodium*

## Cooking Basics

### THE MANY COLORS OF PASTAS & THEIR SAUCES

Not so long ago, pastas came in one color: white with a golden hue. Today, dozens of different ingredients color up and flavor up pastas, often on display in gourmet markets and pasta shops. Each seems to work best with certain types of sauces.

**GREEN MEANS SPINACH**
As its name suggests, green pasta is made by the pasta maker (or you at home) by adding finely chopped spinach to the dough. Best with a rich cream or cheese sauce or chopped fresh tomato.

**RED SAYS TOMATO**
When the dough is made for tomato pasta, concentrated tomato paste is added, turning the dough a vivid orange-red. Almost any sauce works well, especially a green pesto.

**IN THE PINK**
Beet pasta is often made at home, by adding finely chopped beets to the pasta dough. They turn the pasta pink as it bubbles and boils in the pot. Great with creamy cheese sauces.

**BLACK IS SQUID**
Squid ink turns pasta a dramatic black. Try vodka or lemon sauce.

## Cheesy Pasta & Bean Bake

*Prep* **12 MINUTES** *Cook/Bake* **55 MINUTES**

- 1 pound penne (pens)
- 1 can (16 ounces) diced tomatoes
- 2 cans (16 ounces each) kidney beans, drained and rinsed
- 1 jar (26 ounces) pasta sauce
- 8 ounces shredded mozzarella cheese (2 cups)

*Together, pasta and beans form a complex carbohydrate, which is a mix of ingredients that is chock full of vitamins and minerals.*

**LET'S BEGIN** Preheat the oven to 375°F. Prepare the pasta according to package directions. Drain and return to the pot. Mix in the tomatoes, beans, and pasta sauce. Transfer to an 11 × 7-inch baking dish and sprinkle with the cheese.

**INTO THE OVEN** Bake for 40 minutes, or until the cheese has melted and turned golden.

***Makes 6 to 8 servings***

*Per serving: 672 calories, 28g protein, 107g carbohydrates, 15g fat, 7g saturated fat, 29mg cholesterol, 1,473mg sodium*

## Stuffed Shells with Three Cheeses

*Prep* **15 MINUTES** *Cook/Bake* **40 MINUTES**

- 18 jumbo pasta shells
- 1 container (15 ounces) ricotta cheese
- 1 package (10 ounces) frozen chopped broccoli, thawed and well drained
- 1 cup shredded mozzarella cheese
- ⅓ cup grated Parmesan cheese
- ¼ teaspoon ground pepper
- 1 jar (28 ounces) pasta sauce with garden vegetables

*Look for the biggest shells you can find for this recipe. Be certain to cover them completely with sauce and cheese before baking.*

**LET'S BEGIN** Preheat the oven to 400°F. Cook the pasta according to package directions. Drain and keep warm. Meanwhile, stir the ricotta, broccoli, ½ cup of the mozzarella, the Parmesan, and pepper together in a medium bowl.

**COMBINE AND STUFF** Spoon 2 tablespoons of the filling into each shell. Spread 1 cup of the pasta sauce in a 13 × 9-inch baking dish. Arrange the shells in the sauce in one layer. Pour over remaining sauce. Sprinkle with rest of mozzarella.

**INTO THE OVEN** Bake for 25 minutes, or until hot.

***Makes 6 servings***

*Per serving: 400 calories, 20g protein, 40g carbohydrates, 18g fat, 9g saturated fat, 54mg cholesterol, 790mg sodium*

# Creamy Crab-Stuffed Shells

*Prep* **30 MINUTES** *Cook/Bake* **35 MINUTES**

- 24 to 30 jumbo pasta shells
- 3 tablespoons margarine
- 1 tablespoon finely chopped green bell pepper
- 1 tablespoon finely chopped red onion
- 12 ounces crabmeat
- ½ teaspoon ground black pepper
- 1 teaspoon Old Bay seasoning
- 1 large egg, lightly beaten
- 2 cups nonfat milk
- ½ cup low-fat mayonnaise
- 2 tablespoons all-purpose flour
- ½ cup grated Parmesan cheese

*Plan ahead: stuff the pasta shells up in the morning and refrigerate.*

**LET'S BEGIN** Preheat oven to 350°F. Spray bottom of a 13×9-inch baking dish with nonstick cooking spray. Cook the pasta according to package directions. Melt 2 tablespoons of margarine in a small skillet over medium heat. Sauté the green pepper and onion for 4 minutes, or until soft.

**MIX IT UP** Mix crabmeat, pepper, seasoning, egg, 2 tablespoons milk, pepper-onion mixture, and mayonnaise together in a large bowl, then spoon into shells. Put in a baking dish.

**MAKE IT SAUCY** Melt the remaining 2 tablespoons margarine in a medium saucepan over low heat. Whisk in the flour, then gradually whisk in 1½ cups milk, adding remaining milk if needed to make a smooth sauce. Stir in Parmesan and drizzle over shells. Bake for 30 minutes, or until bubbling.

***Makes 6 to 8 servings***

*Per serving: 324 calories, 22g protein, 37g carbohydrates, 11g fat, 3g saturated fat, 91mg cholesterol, 705mg sodium*

# Lasagna Florentine

*Prep* **30 MINUTES** *Cook/Bake* **60 MINUTES**

- 12 lasagna noodles
- 1 container (32 ounces) ricotta cheese
- 2 packages (10 ounces each) frozen chopped spinach, thawed and squeezed dry
- 8 ounces shredded mozzarella cheese (2 cups)
- ½ cup grated Parmesan cheese
- 2 large eggs
- Pinch ground nutmeg (optional)
- 1 jar (32 ounces) pasta sauce with meat

*Dishes à la florentine are "in the style of Florence," as in Italy, and dishes often contain eggs or fish and a layer of spinach.*

**LET'S BEGIN** Preheat the oven to 375°F. Cook the noodles according to package directions. Drain and spread out on kitchen towels in one layer. Combine the ricotta, spinach, mozzarella, ¼ cup of the Parmesan, the eggs, and nutmeg in a large bowl.

**LAYER IT EASY** Spread 1 cup of the pasta sauce on the bottom of a 13×9-inch baking dish. Layer with 4 lasagna noodles and one-half of the spinach mixture, repeating the layers once. Top with the remaining noodles and pasta sauce, then sprinkle with the remaining ¼ cup Parmesan.

**INTO THE OVEN** Cover tightly with foil and bake for 50 minutes. Remove the foil and bake for 10 minutes longer, or until bubbly. Let stand 10 minutes for easier serving.

***Makes 8 servings***

*Per serving: 540 calories, 31g protein, 41g carbohydrates, 28g fat, 15g saturated fat, 141mg cholesterol, 988mg sodium*

## Microwave in Minutes

### REHEAT PASTA FAST!

Your microwave is invaluable when reheating pasta. A small amount of pasta (1 to 2 servings) heats best. Spread out the pasta in a microwavable dish, sprinkle with a few drops of water and cover partially with plastic wrap (do not seal tightly). Microwave on High for about 1 minute. Toss with a fork. If all of the pasta is not warm yet, continue heating at 15-second intervals on High.

**Tip:** If you're reheating more than 2 servings of pasta, it's easier and faster to drop the cooked pasta into boiling water on the top of the stove for a minute or two.

# Vegetable Pasta Bake

*Prep* **15 MINUTES** *Bake* **25 MINUTES**

- 3 cups mostaccioli (little moustaches), cooked and drained
- 1 jar (27½ ounces) light pasta sauce
- 1 package (8 ounces) 2% shredded reduced-fat mozzarella cheese
- 2 cups thinly sliced mushrooms
- 2 cups yellow squash slices, halved
- 2 cups zucchini slices, halved

*Try substituting blanched carrots for the yellow squash in this dish. Add slivered fresh basil to the sauce.*

**LET'S BEGIN** Preheat the oven to 375°F. Cook the pasta according to package directions. Drain and keep warm.

**MIX IT IN** Mix the pasta, pasta sauce, 1 cup of the cheese, and the vegetables together in a large bowl. Transfer to a 13×9-inch baking dish and sprinkle with the remaining cheese.

**INTO THE OVEN** Bake for 20 to 25 minutes or until heated through.

***Makes 6 servings***

*Per serving: 370 calories, 21g protein, 56g carbohydrates, 7g fat, 4g saturated fat, 20mg cholesterol, 327mg sodium,*

# Rosa's Tuna Lasagna Alfredo

*Prep* **25 MINUTES** *Cook* **45 MINUTES**

- 9 lasagna noodles
- 1 container (15 ounces) ricotta cheese
- 1 package (10 ounces) frozen chopped spinach, thawed and squeezed dry
- ¾ cup grated Parmesan cheese
- 2 scallions, chopped
- 1 large egg, lightly beaten
- 2½ cups pasta sauce
- 1 can (6 ounces) chunk light tuna with a touch of lemon, drained
- 1 cup grated carrots
- 1 cup finely chopped red bell peppers
- 1 container (15 ounces) Alfredo sauce
- 10 ounces shredded mozzarella or provolone cheese (2½ cups)

*Canned tuna is a fabulous convenience food—and everyone loves it! Here, it is the base of a really flavorful lasagna—even better than that ever-loved tuna noodle casserole.*

**LET'S BEGIN** Preheat the oven to 375°F. Cook the noodles according to package directions. Drain and place on a kitchen towel in one layer. Combine the ricotta, spinach, ½ cup of the Parmesan, the scallions, and egg in a medium bowl.

**LAYER IT EASY** Spread 1 cup of the pasta sauce in the bottom of a 13 × 9-inch baking dish. Layer with 3 noodles, one-half the ricotta mixture, the tuna, carrots, bell pepper, and Alfredo sauce, then sprinkle with 1 cup of the mozzarella. Repeat the layers once. Top with 1½ cups of the pasta sauce.

**INTO THE OVEN** Bake for 30 minutes, then sprinkle with the remaining mozzarella. Bake for 5 minutes longer, or until the cheese melts. Let stand for 10 minutes for easier serving.

***Makes 12 servings***

*Per serving: 370 calories, 19g protein, 29g carbohydrates, 20g fat, 10g saturated fat, 80mg cholesterol, 752mg sodium*

# CREDITS

**PAGE 2** Kraft Foods: Photo for Triple-Pepper Fettuccine courtesy of Kraft Kitchens. Used with permission.

**PAGE 8** Lawry's: Photo for Michael's Pasta courtesy of Lawry's Foods. Used with permission.

**PAGE 13** Lawry's: Photo for Fettuccine Salad courtesy of Lawry's Foods. Used with permission.

**PAGE 16** Del Monte: Photo for Tortellini with Tomatoes & Zucchini courtesy of Del Monte Foods. Used with permission.

**PAGE 18** National Pasta Association: Recipe for Flash Primavera courtesy of the National Pasta Association. Used with permission.

**PAGE 19** Bertolli: Recipe for Pasta with Proscuitto & Vegetables courtesy of Unilever Bestfoods North America. Used with permission.

**PAGE 20** Bertolli: Recipe for Rigatoni in Vodka Sauce courtesy of Unilever Bestfoods North America. Used with permission.

**PAGE 20** National Association of Margarine Manufacturers: Recipe for Lemon Pasta courtesy of the National Association of Margarine Manufacturers. Used with permission.

**PAGE 21** Lawry's: Recipe and photo for Hot & Spicy Broccoli Beef courtesy of Lawry's Foods. Used with permission.

**PAGE 22/23** National Pork Board: Recipe and photo for Rigatoni with Olives & Bacon courtesy of the National Pork Board. Used with permission.

**PAGE 23** National Pork Board: Recipe for Pork & Pasta Skillet Supper courtesy of the National Pork Board. Used with permission.

**PAGE 24** Del Monte: Recipe for Tortellini with Tomatoes & Zucchini courtesy of Del Monte Foods.

**PAGE 25** National Pasta Association: Recipe and photo for Pasta with Homemade Meat Sauce courtesy of the National Pasta Association. Used with permission.

**PAGE 26** Kraft Foods: Recipe and photo for Lasagna Rolls courtesy of Kraft Kitchens. Used with permission.

**PAGE 27** Kikkoman: Recipe for Quick Chili Mac courtesy of Kikkoman. Used with permission.

**PAGE 28** National Pasta Association: Recipe for Lone Star Steak & Pasta courtesy of the National Pasta Association. Used with permission.

**PAGE 29** Campbell Soup Company: Recipe for Easy Beef & Pasta courtesy of Campbell Soup Company

**PAGE 29** McCormick: Recipe for Spaghetti Pie courtesy of McCormick. Used with permission.

**PAGE 30** Ragu: Recipe for Chicken & Linguine in Creamy Tomato Sauce. Taste Tested Recipe from The Ragu Kitchens. Used with permission.

**PAGE 31** Birds Eye: Recipe for Angel Hair with Chicken & Vegetables courtesy of Birds Eye Foods. Used with permission.

**PAGE 32/33** Kraft Foods: Recipe and photo for Shrimp Linguine Primavera courtesy of Kraft Kitchens. Used with permission.

**PAGE 33** Ragu: Recipe for Shrimp Robusto. Taste Tested Recipe from The Ragu Kitchens. Used with permission.

**PAGE 34** Bertolli: Recipe for Easy Linguine with Red Clam Sauce courtesy of Unilever Bestfoods North America. Used with permission.

**PAGE 35** National Pasta Association: Recipe and photo for Pasta Marinara courtesy of the National Pasta Association. Used with permission.

**PAGE 36** Sunkist: Photo for Orange-Lemon Angel Hair Pasta courtesy of Sunkist Growers, Inc. Used with permission.

**PAGE 38** National Pasta Association: Recipe and photo for Zesty California Stuffed Shells courtesy of the National Pasta Association. Used with permission.

**PAGE 39** Kraft Foods: Recipe for Pasta Primavera Alfredo courtesy of Kraft Kitchens. Used with permission.

**PAGE 40/41** Kraft Foods: Recipe and photo for Triple-Pepper Fettuccine courtesy of Kraft Kitchens. Used with permission.

**PAGE 41** Wheat Foods Council: Recipe for Garden-Fresh Pasta courtesy of the Wheat Foods Council. Used with permission.

**PAGE 42** McCormick: Recipe for Magnificent Monterey Pasta courtesy of McCormick. Used with permission.

**PAGE 43** Sunkist: Recipe and photo for Orange-Lemon Angel Hair Pasta courtesy of Sunkist Growers, Inc. Used with permission.

**PAGE 44** Colavita: Recipe for Farfalle Primavera courtesy of Colavita. Used with permission.

**PAGE 45** National Pasta Association: Recipe and photo for Bowties alle Portofino courtesy of the National Pasta Association. Used with permission.

**PAGE 46/47** Lawry's: Recipe and photo for Grilled Tequila Lime Shrimp courtesy of Lawry's Foods. Used with permission.

**PAGE 48** Bumble Bee: Recipe for Spaghetti & Tuna with a Touch of Lemon courtesy of Bumble Bee Seafoods. Used with permission.

**PAGE 49** Ragu: Recipe for Meaty Pasta Ratatouille. Taste Tested Recipe from The Ragu Kitchens. Used with permission.

**PAGE 50** National Pasta Association: Recipe for Pasta with Fresh Salsa courtesy of the National Pasta Association. Used with permission.

**PAGE 51** National Pasta Association: Recipe and photo for Layered Picnic Pasta Salad courtesy of the National Pasta Association. Used with permission.

**PAGE 52/53** National Pork Board: Recipe and photo for Mediterranean Pasta Salad courtesy of the National Pork Board.

**PAGE 54** Perdue: Photo for Italiano Turkey Ravioli courtesy of © Perdue Farms. Used with permission.

**PAGE 56** Wisconsin Milk Marketing Board: Recipe and photo for Classic Mac & Cheese courtesy of the Wisconsin Milk Marketing Board. Used with permission.

**PAGE 57** 8th Continent: Recipe for Macaroni & Three Cheeses courtesy of 8th Continent LLC. 8TH CONTINENT® trademark used with permission.

**PAGE 58** National Pasta Association: Recipe for Creamy Chicken & Mushroom Fettuccine courtesy of the National Pasta Association. Used with permission.

**PAGE 59** Bertolli: Recipe for Pasta with Tomato-Gorgonzola Sauce courtesy of Unilever Bestfoods North America. Used with permission.

**PAGE 60/61** Del Monte: Recipe and photo for Penne with Beans & Tomatoes courtesy of Del Monte Foods. Used with permission.

**PAGE 61** Birds Eye: Recipe for Pasta Primavera with Lemon-Pepper Sauce courtesy of Birds Eye Foods. Used with permission.

**PAGE 62** National Pasta Association: Recipe for Hay & Straw courtesy of the National Pasta Association. Used with permission.

**PAGE 63** Campbell Soup Company: Recipe and photo for 2-Step Cheesy Garlic Twists courtesy of Campbell Soup Company. Used with permission.

**PAGE 64** National Pasta Association: Recipe for Southwestern Spaghetti Pie courtesy of the National Pasta Association. Used with permission.

**PAGE 65** Perdue: Recipe for Italiano Turkey Ravioli courtesy of © Perdue Farms. Used with permission.

**PAGE 66/67** Lawry's: Recipe and photo for Michael's Pasta courtesy of Lawry's Foods. Used with permission.

**PAGE 67** Almond Board of California: Recipe for California Almond Fettuccine courtesy of the Almond Board of California. Used with permission.

**PAGE 68** French's: Recipe for Baked Penne & Ham courtesy of *French's*® French Fried Onions. Used with permission.

**PAGE 69** Birds Eye: Recipe for Fettuccine with Shrimp & Vegetables courtesy of Birds Eye Foods. Used with permission.

**PAGE 70/71** Lawry's: Recipe and photo for Fettuccine Salad courtesy of Lawry's Foods. Used with permission.

**PAGE 72** National Pork Board: Photo for Pork & Noodle Stir-fry courtesy of the National Pork Board. Used with permission.

**PAGE 74/75** Land O'Lakes: Recipe and photo for Seaside Shrimp Linguine courtesy of Land O'Lakes, Inc. Used with permission.

**PAGE 76** National Pasta Association: Recipe and photo for Orzo with Cranberries & Sausage courtesy of the National Pasta Association. Used with permission.

**PAGE 77** Tone Brothers: Recipe for Southwestern Chicken Spaghetti courtesy of Tone Brothers, Inc., producer of Tone's, Spice Islands, and Durkee products. Used with permission.

**PAGE 78** Bertolli: Recipe for Penne Rustica courtesy of Unilever Bestfoods North America. Used with permission.

**PAGE 78** Birds Eye: Recipe for Bowties with Vegetables Alfredo courtesy of Birds Eye Foods. Used with permission.

**PAGE 79** French's: Recipe and photo for Penne with Arrabbiata Sauce courtesy of *Frank's*® *RedHot*® Cayenne Pepper Sauce. Used with permission.

**PAGE 80** National Pasta Association: Recipe and photo for Beer Brat Pasta courtesy of the National Pasta Association. Used with permission.

**PAGE 81** Ragu: Recipe for Tuscan Pasta. Taste Tested Recipe from The Ragu Kitchens. Used with permission.

**PAGE 82** National Pork Board: Recipe and photo for The Other Meatballs & Spaghetti courtesy of the National Pork Board. Used with permission.

**PAGE 83** Mrs. T's Pierogies: Recipe and photo for Shrimp Divine Pierogies courtesy of Mrs. T's Pierogies. Used with permission.

**PAGE 84/85** Land O'Lakes: Recipe and photo for Mushroom Stroganoff courtesy of Land O'Lakes, Inc. Used with permission.

**PAGE 86** The Peanut Institute: Recipe for Pasta Peanut Stir-fry courtesy of The Peanut Institute. Used with permission.

**PAGE 87** National Pork Board: Recipe for Pork & Noodle Stir-fry courtesy of the National Pork Board. Used with permission.

**PAGE 88** Cherry Marketing Institute: Recipe and photo for Couscous Salad with Dried Cherries courtesy of The Cherry Marketing Institute. Used with permission.

**PAGE 89** Kikkoman: Recipe for Sesame-Ginger Noodles courtesy of Kikkoman. Used with permission.

**PAGE 90/91** Kikkoman: Recipe and photo for Snake Alley Noodles courtesy of Kikkoman. Used with permission.

**PAGE 92/93** Kraft Foods: Recipe and photo for Asian Pasta Salad courtesy of Kraft Kitchens. Used with permission.

**PAGE 94/95** National Pork Board: Recipe and photo for Indonesian Pork Noodle Bowl courtesy of the National Pork Board. Used with permission.

**PAGE 96** Perdue: Recipe and photo for Chicken Zorba courtesy of © Perdue Farms. Used with permission.

**PAGE 97** Kraft Foods: Recipe and photo for Asian Chicken 'n' Noodles courtesy of Kraft Kitchens. Used with permission.

**PAGE 98** Kraft Foods: Photo for Bistro Chicken Pasta Salad courtesy of Kraft Kitchens. Used with permission.

**PAGE 100/101** U.S. Apple Association: Recipe and photo for Apple Tortellini Salad courtesy of the U.S. Apple Association. Used with permission.

**PAGE 102** Ocean Spray Cranberries: Recipe for Orzo Salad courtesy of Ocean Spray Cranberries, Inc. Used with permission.

**PAGE 103** Lawry's: Recipe and photo for Grilled Chicken Pasta Toss courtesy of Lawry's Inc. Used with permission.

**PAGE 104/105** Kraft Foods: Recipe and photo for Ravioli Alfredo courtesy of Kraft Kitchens. Used with permission.

**PAGE 106** Birds Eye: Recipe for Ravioli with Creamy Spinach Sauce courtesy of Birds Eye Foods. Used with permission.

**PAGE 107** National Pasta Association: Recipe for Caesar Shrimp & Pasta courtesy of the National Pasta Association. Used with permission.

**PAGE 108/109** Kraft Foods: Recipe and photo for Minestrone Pasta Salad courtesy of Kraft Kitchens. Used with permission.

**PAGE 110/111** Lawry's: Recipe and photo for Pork Linguine Salad courtesy of Lawry's Foods. Used with permission.

**PAGE 112** Kraft Foods: Recipe and photo for Tangy Pasta Salad courtesy of Kraft Kitchens. Used with permission.

**PAGE 113** National Pasta Association: Recipe for Spaghetti with White Clam Sauce courtesy of the National Pasta Association. Used with permission.

**PAGE 114** McIlhenny Company: Recipe and photo for Shrimp & Artichoke Linguine courtesy of McIlhenny Company. Used with permission.

**PAGE 115** California Walnut Marketing Board: Recipe and photo for Broccoli-Walnut Noodles courtesy of The California Walnut Marketing Board. Used with permission.

**PAGE 116** Kraft Foods: Recipe and photo for Bistro Chicken Pasta Salad courtesy of Kraft Kitchens. Used with permission.

**PAGE 117** National Pasta Association: Recipe and photo for Pasta with Turkey Sausage & Olives courtesy of the National Pasta Association. Used with permission.

**PAGE 118/119** National Pork Board: Recipe and photo for Citrus-Cherry Pork & Pasta Salad courtesy of the National Pork Board. Used with permission.

**PAGE 120/121** McCormick: Recipe and photo for Italian Chicken Pasta courtesy of McCormick. Used with permission.

**PAGE 122/123** National Chicken Council: Recipe and photo for Reunion Pasta Salad courtesy of the National Chicken Council/U.S. Poultry & Egg Association. Used with permission.

**PAGE 123** French's: Recipe for Best-Ever Macaroni Salad courtesy of *French's*® mustard. Used with permission.

**PAGE 124/125** Land O'Lakes: Recipe and photo for Vegetable Linguine with Peanut Sauce courtesy of Land O'Lakes, Inc. Used with permission.

**PAGE 126** Kraft Foods: Photo for Four-Cheese Broccoli Bake courtesy of Kraft Kitchens. Used with permission.

**PAGE 128** Ragu: Recipe for No-Boil Lasagna. Taste Tested Recipe from The Ragu Kitchens. Used with permission.

**PAGE 129** Kraft Foods: Recipe for Easy Classic Lasagna courtesy of Kraft Kitchens. Used with permission.

**PAGE 130** National Pasta Association: Recipe for Iron Skillet Spaghetti courtesy of the National Pasta Association. Used with permission.

**PAGE 131** Cherry Marketing Institute: Recipe and photo for Beef Burgundy courtesy of The Cherry Marketing Institute. Used with permission.

**PAGE 132** Ragu: Recipe for No-Boil Ziti. Taste Tested Recipe from The Ragu Kitchens. Used with permission.

**PAGE 132/133** Kraft Foods: Recipe and photo for Beef & Mozzarella Pie courtesy of Kraft Kitchens. Used with permission.

**PAGE 134** Kraft Foods: Recipe for Four-Cheese Broccoli Bake courtesy of Kraft Kitchens. Used with permission.

**PAGE 135** Bush's Best Beans: Recipe for Cheesy Pasta & Bean Bake courtesy of Bush's Best® Beans. Used with permission.

**PAGE 135** Campbell Soup Company: Recipe for Stuffed Shells with Three Cheeses courtesy of Campbell Soup Company. Used with permission.

**PAGE 136** National Pasta Association: Recipe and photo for Creamy Crab-stuffed Shells courtesy of the National Pasta Association. Used with permission.

**PAGE 137** Ragu: Recipe for Lasagne Florentine. Taste Tested Recipe from The Ragu Kitchens. Used with permission.

**PAGE 138** Kraft Foods: Recipe and photo for Vegetable Pasta Bake courtesy of Kraft Kitchens. Used with permission.

**PAGE 139** Bumble Bee: Recipe and photo for Rosa's Tuna Lasagna Alfredo courtesy of Bumble Bee Seafoods. Used with permission.

# Websites

**RODALE INC.**
www.rodale.com

Almond Board of California
www.AlmondsAreIn.com

Bertolli
www.Bertolli.com

Birds Eye
www.birdseyefoods.com

Bumble Bee
www.bumblebee.com

Bush's Best Beans
www.bushbeans.com

California Walnut Marketing Board
www.walnuts.org

Campbell Soup Company
www.campbellskitchen.com

Cherry Marketing Institute
www.usacherries.com

Colavita
www.colavita.com

Del Monte
www.delmonte.com

8th Continent
www.8thcontinent.com

French's & Red Hot
www.frenchsfoods.com

Kikkoman
www.kikkoman-usa.com

Kraft Foods
www.kraftfoods.com

Land O'Lakes
www.landolakes.com

Lawry's
www.lawrys.com

McCormick
www.mccormick.com

McIlhenny Company
www.tabasco.com

Mrs. T's Pierogies
www.pierogies.com

National Association of Margarine Manufacturers
www.margarine.org

National Chicken Council
www.eatchicken.com

National Pasta Association
www.ilovepasta.org

National Pork Board
www.otherwhitemeat.com

Ocean Spray Cranberries
www.oceanspray.com

Perdue
www.perdue.com

Ragu
www.eat.com

Sunkist
www.sunkist.com

The Peanut Institute
www.peanut-institute.org

Tone Brothers
www.spiceadvice.com

U.S. Apple Association
www.usapple.org

Wheat Foods Council
www.wheatfoods.org

Wisconsin Milk Marketing Board
www.wisdairy.com

# INDEX

✔ Designates a SuperQuick recipe that gets you in and out of the kitchen in 30 minutes or less!
*Italic* page numbers refer to boxed text. **Bold** faced page numbers refer to photographs.